THE R

English nationalism and the
transformation of working-class politics

Simon Winlow, Steve Hall and
James Treadwell

P

First published in Great Britain in 2017 by

Policy Press
University of Bristol
1-9 Old Park Hill
Bristol
BS2 8BB
UK
t: +44 (0)117 954 5940
pp-info@bristol.ac.uk
www.policypress.co.uk

North America office:
Policy Press
c/o The University of Chicago Press
1427 East 60th Street
Chicago, IL 60637, USA
t: +1 773 702 7700
f: +1 773 702 9756
sales@press.uchicago.edu
www.press.uchicago.edu

British Library Cataloguing in Publication Data
A catalogue record for this book is available from the British Library.

Library of Congress Cataloging-in-Publication Data
A catalog record for this book has been requested.

ISBN 9978-1-4473-2848-3 paperback
ISBN 978-1-4473-2851-3 ePub
ISBN 978-1-4473-2852-0 Mobi
ISBN 978-1-4473-2850-6 ePdf

The right of Simon Winlow, Steve Hall and James Treadwell to be identified as the authors of this work has been asserted by them in accordance with the Copyright, Designs and Patents Act 1988.

Cover design by Soapbox design
Front cover: image kindly supplied by Getty
Printed and bound in Great Britain by TJ International, Padstow
Policy Press uses environmentally responsible print partners

Contents

ONE

Introduction

Je ne sais quoi…

This book is based on the conviction that an honest, detailed and contextualised analysis of the rise of English nationalism among the working class can shed light on the unpredictable and volatile times in which we live. Lately we have witnessed some of the most profound shifts in the history of political economy. Neoliberalism's global economic logic has established itself as the dominant organising principle in our lives. All known alternative modes of socioeconomic organisation have disintegrated and virtually disappeared from everyday practice and the popular imagination. In such a political hiatus neoliberalism has pressed on unhindered with the deindustrialisation of many areas of Europe and North America and the rapid industrialisation of China and other parts of the developing world. In many regions of the deindustrialised west we have seen the gap between rich and poor grow to historic proportions in a realigned social structure that can now be legitimately described as a plutocracy (Winlow and Hall, 2013; Dorling, 2014; Therborn, 2014). We have also seen global warming, drought, mass migration and the depletion of many of the natural resources that are vital to the uninterrupted economic growth on which the functioning of the capitalist system and the livelihoods of its subjects depend (Klare, 2008; Heinberg, 2011; Hiscock, 2012).

Our political culture has grown sterile. It no longer appears to be capable of engaging the people in an informed and forthright discussion about root-and-branch changes to the way we live together. The vast majority of our politicians display a

1

dispiriting lack of will to challenge and overcome the historic problems we face. Most have accepted the transformation of the old modernist social order, with its unequal yet stable and comprehensible structure of entitlements and obligations, into a world of hollow freedoms, insecurity and panoramic dissatisfaction. The new political consensus has been forged in a silent pact between the liberal left and the neoliberal right, a dual power bloc that looks down on the corpses of socialism and one-nation conservatism (Rancière, 2010a, 2010b). This tacit agreement, built on an unwavering commitment to the free market, has opened a gap between institutionalised politics and the cultural life of the people. The political establishment no longer speaks to the experiences, hopes and dreams óf ordinary people, and dismisses all their fears, no matter how grounded they might be, as irrational and counterproductive to the continued flourishing of progressive cultural life. It is increasingly devoid of the grand visions of fundamental socioeconomic transformation that once made politics real and capable of even modestly and incrementally delivering on the promises made to men and women across the country.

Any honest appraisal of recent times in the west must acknowledge that out there in the real world exists a surfeit of anxiety. We, as a nation, as a culture, as inhabitants of this moribund post-political epoch, appear significantly less sure of ourselves than the generation that emerged from the horrors of the first half of the 20th century to take on the challenges of building a new society among the ruins of the old. We appear to have woken up from the modernist dreams of incremental social improvement into the pervasive cynicism of neoliberal reality. We worry about what lies in store for us, and what lies in store for our children and grandchildren. Despite an abundance of consumer goods and lives full of a million things we must do, in many parts of the west there is an almost palpable sense of lack. Huge numbers from across the social spectrum seem to be in search of some missing object or force that, were it to suddenly reappear, could set matters straight and enable a new positive mood to develop. A general sense that things are not quite right hangs like a pall in the air.

However, we cannot quite manage to identify precisely what is missing, and what might be causing this vague but enduring discomfort. In making this claim some may accuse us of being unnecessarily bleak. However, this bleakness is inextricably tied to the subject matter of this book. As we will see, there are many ordinary people out there who have an even bleaker outlook. They often see for themselves a life of unending struggle, a life in which the pleasures of community life have been withdrawn, a life of frustration, interrupted all too briefly by occasional flurries of consumerist hedonism. They can sense life only as a backward step, the loss of things deemed valuable and important. The benefits of our allegedly open, marketised society are the privileges of successful others. Those trapped in the lower echelons can see no forward step in their own lives. They are convinced that for them the best times have now been left behind. Things are trending downwards.

As a result of all this, a growing number of these people are now very angry. What they lack is not simply absent. Rather, it has been purposefully removed, appropriated by competitive others keen to secure their own interests. Occasional bursts of happiness and charitable fellow-feeling do little to dispel an obdurate sense of coming crisis, of things wearing away, of rootlessness and loss. Despite the proliferation of affordable consumer goods, advances in technology, the onward march of scientific discovery, improved healthcare, the spread of democracy and great strides made in the tolerance and celebration of difference in culture, sexuality, ethnicity, religion and lifestyle, a shared anxiety about the future and what it may have in store for us cannot be appeased. This malaise is not simply the outcome of marginalisation. It is not simply something that affects those at the very bottom. Even those who appear to us as the great winners of our time seem unable to understand their lives in wholly positive terms. We are all living through a time of great wealth and relative cultural freedom, but despite this, many carry this sense of foreboding. Underneath all the surface freedoms lies a deeper sense of fatalism and lassitude, a sense that something better could exist but does not, and in all likelihood, never will.

While we all tend to acknowledge that there is likely to be some unknown negativity lurking out there in the shadows, for many this awareness is too disturbing to face head on. All awareness of a coming crisis is disavowed and blocked from consciousness. They know, but they do not want to know, so they continue onward as if they are not in possession of this knowledge. It is repressed and seeks its return in other forms disconnected from the underlying set of causes and conditions that gave birth to the crisis. Why think too much and too deeply? What good does it do? No one else appears to be particularly concerned, and what can one individual really achieve these days? Accept the world as it is, and try to make the best of things.

The commercialisation of all popular culture might indeed be crass, but it functions well enough to draw our attention away from the real world, with all its manifold pathologies. Porn, talent shows, reality TV, social networking, gambling. Foreign holidays, celebrity gossip, a big Saturday night out on the town. Lager, weed, coke, speed, sex, takeaway food. Valium, Xanax, Citalopram, Fluoxetine, Prozac. Of course, we can occupy our time in what appear more wholesome ways. Shopping, cooking, sport, DIY, gardening, hobbies. We try to keep busy in ways that suit our personal interests. We fill our days with activities to cover up our deeper inaction, our inability to truly strike out and address those things that must be addressed if genuine progress is to be made. Not that we don't want progress. We occasionally give a few thoughts to vicarious action. We wait for someone or some authoritative body to take measures on our behalf, but our cynicism acts against whatever faith we might still have in transformative politics and the elites who currently dominate our world. We don't really expect too much. That's because everything is flawed. Everything is in some way sullied. We have nothing left to believe in, except our cynical non-belief. Dark thoughts continue to lurk at the edge of consciousness. They press forward in the downtime and demand recognition. They cannot be held at bay forever.

This sense of lack, this sense that something is missing, that something valuable and important has been lost, discarded or stolen from us — and is therefore no longer accessible to the very communities and individuals most in need of it — exists as a general background to our study. Occasionally this sense of lack migrates to the foreground to be discussed directly by members of the working class who have taken up the nationalist cause. However, for the most part, it stays in the background, framing foreground events and casting them in its shadow.

It didn't have to be this way...

We hope to carry you, the reader, into the lifeworld of the EDL, and the cultural context that gave birth to it. First, we must warn you that this world is bleak. It does not inspire optimism, that comforting but often politically destructive quality that some readers demand the writer should provide as a matter of duty. Rather, our goal is to enable you, however briefly, to see the world as EDL supporters see it. We also hope to identify the fundamental forces that have encouraged these men and women to adopt such a crude, forthright and hostile worldview. You may find some of this story disturbing, or at least disconcerting. Some will no doubt decline to pick up this book, convinced that we know as much as we need to know about these retrograde fascists. Some will claim that writing about them gives them the attention, publicity and credibility they don't deserve. But those who simply oppose what they do not understand are running away from the political reality of our times. If social scientists are to assist in the task of making sense of that reality, we can't simply restrict ourselves to the nice topics. We can't simply praise the nice people and condemn the bad. We have to go deeper. We have to expose ourselves to challenging topics, and we have to be honest about what we find. So, this book presents material that some will find unpalatable. We will also develop an analysis that could make many on the political and academic left feel uncomfortable, and perhaps mildly aggrieved. No matter. We will report the world as we found it, and we will explain that world in a manner that seems to us useful and appropriate.

For the moment, however, looking back on our two decades of grounded social research with the scattered remnants of England's old white working class, only one thought is uppermost in our minds: it didn't have to be this way. Things could have been so much better, for all of us, and that includes those who have drifted into the dark space occupied by the EDL.

All that said, our analysis should not cast us all into a pit of despair. Nor should it supply unwanted credibility to the dangerous politics of the far right. While our story is often sad, frustrating and worrisome, we remain convinced that only by acknowledging and coming to terms with the worst of our times will a new political movement arise capable of setting matters straight. The reality of the social forces that constitute the EDL are analogous to the physical forces that cause global warming – both stem from activities and events that have already taken place. We have no choice but to deal with the consequences. Nationalism is on the rise across the continent. A large and growing number of working-class men and women feel aggrieved. They feel ignored by mainstream politics. This is a reality, and it makes no sense to deny it. The first step is to reach down to understand what was behind these activities and events in the first place.

What is the English Defence League?

Make no mistake, the EDL represents a misguided attempt to respond politically to the enduring sense of diminishment and lack we have described above. It attempts to restore what has been lost and defend what remains. It hopes to rebuild foundations, and clear away the miasma of fakery and doubt that hangs over our culture. Analysts are right to suggest that far right movements furnish their members with a sense of purpose and possibility (Busher, 2015), but why should people need this in what we are constantly told is a healthy, functioning democracy? Gradually, dissatisfaction with what exists is slowly pushing individuals back on to the political field. However, ideology has changed, and the established ideological platforms of modern political movements no longer exist in the way they once did. Inevitably, in such a hiatus, there is, as Tilly (2008) suggests, an air of improvisation to contemporary working-class politics.

The EDL is, of course, a fringe political group cut adrift from mainstream politics and overtly antagonistic to many of the central concerns of contemporary liberal multiculturalism. The group has no system of formal membership. Rather, it attracts supporters who sympathise with the EDL's core principles and goals, the majority of whom drift in and out of its activities. However, despite its fragile and sporadic existence, it maintains core principles founded on a dissatisfaction with immigration policies and a desire to mobilise against the spread of what it sees as the hostile alien culture of radical Islamism. It hopes to defend the interests of the native population from the perceived threats posed by immigrants, multiculturalism and what it imagines to be the growing power and paramilitary forms of the Muslim faith in England.

EDL supporters are also angry about the power of metropolitan liberalism and its co-option of the parliamentary system. They are angry because this elite has, in recent years, seen fit to open the borders of Britain to wave after wave of immigration. They are angry because too little has been done to defend the economic and cultural entitlements of the white working class, and they are angry about the 'political correctness' they see as a means of systematically avoiding crucial debates about immigration, ethnic diversity and religious antagonism. They are angry at the perceived capitulation of Westminster to radical Islam at home and abroad, they are angry that our armed forces are not adequately supported and championed, and they are angry at what they perceive to be the gradual dilution of traditional English culture and society.

The street protest is The EDL's principal political activity. They have only the vaguest plans to impact upon the government's policy agenda, and, despite the passionate intensity of their protests, the organisation appears almost totally devoid of revolutionary fervour or a desire for significant structural change. We were unable to detect among EDL supporters any great aspiration to formalise the group, or to transform it into an actual political party. It has no clear hierarchy, and, regionally, those who are identified as 'leaders' tend simply to be those who have been most active in organising protests and meetings. EDL supporters do, however, have an active presence on the internet, especially on social networking sites. Their utopianism, where it exists at all, is vaguely 'conservative' in the rather muddled sense that could sometimes be found in traditional working-class culture, and tends to concern itself with the inviolability of their own 'values' and community life.

While the EDL might on the surface display some of the hallmarks of traditional fascism or Nazism, it also displays a number of significant characteristics that set it apart from these older political forms. For example, many EDL supporters actually speak in support of the Jewish faith and the rights of Israel to defend itself against the perceived aggression of Palestine and neighbouring Islamic states.

While much of the academic literature tells us that the cultural and religious conflicts of today tend to be rooted in regressive forms of bigotry and hatred, such logic fails to represent the reality and historical causes of such conflict. Reducing the complexities of systematised and institutionalised conflict to basic emotional states is too simplistic. However, if we must persevere with such logic, we should note that hatred is, in fact, not the dominant emotion displayed by EDL supporters. While some did express what appeared to be a genuine hatred of radical Islamism, *inarticulate anger* was the basic emotion that appeared to typify the EDL's cultural and political life. Those we spoke to were complex individuals fully capable of feeling and expressing a broad range of emotions and sentiments. However, when we attempted to talk to our respondents in everyday social settings about what we might broadly conceive as political issues, anger that was entirely disconnected from the causes of their parlous socioeconomic position came quickly to the fore.

This palpable sense of underlying and very potent yet inarticulate anger begs a series of questions that structure the argument we develop in this book. The most important are these: What is the EDL angry about? Where does this anger come from, and how do EDL supporters justify and explain it? What is it about Islam, Islamic culture and the realities of Muslim community life that makes everything Islamic the primary object of anger? And why do EDL supporters express their anger in the way they do? Why do they focus on street protests, and why do they not, as a group, engage with the established structures of parliamentary democracy?

Once was England

From the outset it is important to note that the EDL draws the overwhelming majority of its support from Britain's old white working class. While traditional nationalism attracted individuals from all classes, the EDL is, unequivocally, a working-class political movement. In making this claim we are not attempting to pathologise the white working class. Rather, we are simply stating a fact that has been made clear to us during our years of fieldwork. We do not deny that the EDL has a few middle-class supporters. However, the EDL's core support is unmistakably working class. All of those we spoke to displayed the traditional characteristics of white working-class identity and culture.

Our fieldwork was generally conducted in the spaces of contemporary white working-class cultural life. We spent a lot of time in pubs, from the ubiquitous corporate bars of the city centre to neighbourhood boozers on sprawling council estates. We also spent time in the homes of our respondents, and often walked with them around their neighbourhoods. We sat around drinking mugs of tea in greasy spoon cafes, we accompanied our respondents to the bookies, and stood chatting with them on street corners and outside pubs and shops. On Saturdays we often headed off to the football. Certainly, we did not encounter any EDL supporters who identified themselves as middle or upper class. More importantly, many of our contacts were animated by issues connected to the contemporary politics of class. Time and time again we were told that the EDL's cause was to protect the cultural and economic interests of England's forgotten white working class.

These men and women are often depicted as unseemly and hostile provocateurs, disrupting an otherwise civilised and hospitable multiethnic urban culture, but to them, their actions were essentially defensive in nature. When they imagined themselves to be moving forward politically, they believed that they were moving forward to reclaim something that had been taken away from them.

Our respondents articulated a general 'politics of us', and in some cases, although certainly not all, this 'politics of us' appeared quite cogent, and reasonably well informed about recent changes to working-class cultural and economic life. Many were quite clearly bonded to their communities, and believed themselves to be standing up to defend these communities from powerful external threats. They spoke at length about the rise of radical Islam and the ubiquitous terrorist threat. They spoke about the involvement of Muslim men in the sexual exploitation of vulnerable young white girls. They spoke about Sharia law and their unwillingness to yield a single additional yard on the field of cultural politics. And when they spoke about these things, they spoke in a forthright manner that reflected their desire to push past the cloying cultural sensitivities that have grown around the popular discussion of immigration, ethnic conflict and religious diversity. We will excavate the foundations of these motivations and explanations as the book develops.

The sentiments and discourse behind the EDL are connected to the concrete localised consequences of the changing economic and cultural circumstances of the white working class. In their rush to condemn the EDL's politics, many liberal commentators omit this crucial and perfectly obvious fact. Many of our respondents talked in detail about the accumulating problems they faced as they tried to reproduce a reasonably safe and secure life for themselves and their families. They talked about declining job prospects, job insecurity, low pay and the difficulties of meeting what they considered to be their basic economic obligations. They believed that the politicians of Westminster and the elites of the big city considered the white working class superfluous in a rapidly changing global economy. They believed that, as a class, they had been, and continue to be, downwardly mobile in economic terms, and vilified, excluded and silenced in cultural terms. They were being overtaken by new economic migrants who were playing the system, and mainstream politicians were complicit in the gradual degradation of the neighbourhoods and life chances of the working class. These things bothered our respondents greatly, and other more specific complaints, frustrations and dissatisfactions merged with these issues to supply energy to the EDL's angry critique of politics. Class identity and class interests were, from the outset, of great importance in the EDL's account of itself, and it was immediately clear to us that any attempt to explain the politics of the EDL must position class centrally in its analysis.

We have no desire to produce yet another descriptive account of the changing class system and the life chances of the white working class, and nor will we reduce the rise of the EDL to the economic instability caused by fundamental changes made to global political economy in the neoliberal era. These issues are important as primary conditions in which anger becomes a probability for those who suffer the worst consequences of this epochal shift, but they cannot, by themselves, explain why the EDL developed when it did and in the manner it did. By itself, an analysis of economic change and the systemic decline of Britain's productivist full employment economy will shed little light on the reasons why Islam became an object of hatred for the EDL. To make sense of these issues we will wander quite far from the usual analytical track, and use a range of materials, concepts and ideas that have hitherto not been deployed in historical accounts of the far right in England. We will address changes in culture, politics and the economy, and connect these changes to the lifeworlds of the white working class.

There is no 'natural' connection between working-class life and right-wing politics. It is worth stressing again that the gradual decline of economic opportunities does not lead inevitably to racism and the politics of nation. Nor should we simply assume that the politics of the far right are a timeless feature of working-class life, and that the popularity of the far right among members of the white working class rises or falls as political circumstances change. The EDL is not simply a slightly updated and repackaged version of the British National Party (BNP), the National Front (NF), the British Union of Fascists (BUF) or any of the other far-right political groups that briefly entered popular consciousness during the 20th century. The EDL differs from all these groups in a number of very important ways. Its sentiments and discourse are connected to issues that are particular to the present epoch. The connections that exist between class, economic life and nationalist politics are complex, and we will work hard in this book to identify the key forces that have pushed these men and women to form such a pugnacious and broadly reviled social movement.

The transformation of working-class politics

There is an underlying concern that sets the context for this racist turn. This is what tends to be absent in contemporary analysis and commentary, but for us, and, as we shall find out later, for the EDL, this is the crux of the matter. Our research experiences and our data have encouraged us to connect the rise of the EDL to a fundamental transformation that has occurred within working-class politics. The locales in which we conducted our research were once the seedbeds of the democratic socialist left in Britain. Most of these areas continue to have a representative from the Labour Party as their Member of Parliament (MP). However, support for the Labour Party has dwindled significantly in recent years, as support for the far right has increased. The United Kingdom Independence Party (UKIP) has been the principal beneficiary of this shift, although Britain's 'first past the post' electoral system has ensured that large numbers of UKIP votes have not yet translated into a large number of UKIP seats in Parliament. And the discourse of the EDL, built on fear of and antagonism towards immigrants, has also achieved a good deal of success in these places.

In areas dominated by the white working class there is a great deal of open discussion of the problems caused by immigrants. We should not assume that only a vocal but relatively insignificant minority hold such views. The reality is much more complicated. Some recent newspaper reports have suggested that the EDL is a spent force and that it can now, in 2015, call upon only a small number of dedicated activists. However, our research suggested quite clearly that in some white working-class areas anti-Muslim and anti-immigrant sentiments are remarkably common. As we will discover, the EDL is not as cohesive as it once was, but this is a relatively minor issue. Of far more importance are the strident anti-immigrant and anti-Muslim sentiments of the EDL's active and inactive supporters, and the sense of common cause that has politicised so many members of the white working class. Are we to believe that anti-immigrant feeling has dissipated because fewer men are turning up at EDL rallies? Are we to believe that the men who were once determined advocates of the EDL have recognised the error of their ways and are now committed to multiculturalism and the basic principles of liberal society? The EDL as an organisation is much less important than the broad and deep 'structure of feeling' in which it is embedded. Falling turnouts at rallies and the apparent splintering of the EDL into different factions and off-shoots are of little importance in comparison to the widespread, enduring and entrenched anti-Muslim sentiments expressed and reproduced in some white working-class neighbourhoods, and of no importance at all to the rapid evaporation of socioeconomic security and the withdrawal of substantive political representation that underpins it. Our attention is therefore directed towards these specific neighbourhoods and the various racisms and antagonisms to be found there.

The journey to the right

After dealing with a number of issues related to the changing nature of working-class politics and the EDL's identification of the Muslim immigrant as a figure of hatred, we move towards what is, for us, perhaps the central conundrum behind the EDL's rise and a crucial motivation for writing this book: why have many white working-class areas become alienated from left-wing politics? Why has recent economic turmoil led to a surge of support for the political right rather than the political left? What has prompted the breakdown of the historic relationship between the political left and the working class? Why is it that, at this specific point in our history, Muslim immigrants and Muslim communities, some of which tend to occupy a roughly similar economic stratum to the white working class and share many of their difficulties, have been identified as objects of hatred?

If we are to understand the EDL we must position it within a specific historical conjuncture. In the early years of the 21st century – years in which a growing antagonism towards Muslim immigrants really began to take hold in some white working-class neighbourhoods – politicians, newspaper columnists, news broadcasters and academics stopped talking about capitalism. Capitalism had become so triumphant, ubiquitous and unchallengeable that it was commonly understood as a non-ideological fact of life. Capitalism had become the only game in town. No feasible and appealing alternative could be imagined. Magically, and right before our eyes, capitalism, with all its stark contradictions and injustices, metamorphosed into 'the economy', a pragmatic, unproblematic and uncontested model for growth and the incremental improvement of lifestyles. The EDL was not and is not concerned with capitalism, and has no desire to regulate or manage it in a way that would secure the relative prosperity of England's white working class. However, the supremacy of the market inevitably forms a significant part of our story. Its supremacy sets the scene by disinvesting in British industry and destabilising traditional working-class labour and community life, which contextualises the political and cultural concerns of the EDL. Consciously, the EDL has no great desire to intervene in socially destructive market forces to restore what has been lost, but its politics are inextricably bound up with the transformation of capitalism and the evaporation of the mainstream political will to regulate or replace it.

In these years the politics of the left underwent a sea–change. Few politicians dared go beyond the tentative suggestion that more money should be spent on welfare. Virtually no one argued for a return to the systematically redistributive politics of social democracy, and not a single soul was willing to propose that we ditch capitalism altogether to develop and adopt a more inclusive economic model. Talking about this too clearly and too loudly could hamper the individual's career as a politician or a researcher and educator. The gap between the Labour Party and the Conservative Party narrowed significantly as both became ever more dedicated to market principles and stoical about even the most destructive of market outcomes, always keen to trade them off ideologically against market benefits. By the 1990s the Labour Party no longer seemed to be associated with the traditional working class or representative of their interests. All political parties, and the metropolitan elites that dominated popular cultural production, were fully signed-up advocates of liberal multiculturalism. At least on the surface of things.

From the very start of the neoliberal era we've seen a gradual reduction in the number of traditional working-class jobs. In their place have risen new and unstable labour markets, mostly in the low-grade service sector. These are low-paid, non-unionised and often part-time jobs that have none of the positive symbolism associated with traditional working-class labour (see Lloyd, 2013). Zero-hours contracts are now normalised, and the general public have become remarkably acclimatised to the precariousness of 21st-century economic life. It's just the way things are these days (see McKenzie, 2015).

However, during these years, before the crash of 2008, relentless 24-hour news broadcasts told the people that the economy was growing at a rapid pace. Many wondered, justifiably, when this good news would translate into significant improvements in their own lifestyles. Inevitably, many ordinary people concluded that the neoliberal economic miracle would never deliver on its promise. The dream life of wealth, glamour and freedom they saw on TV – beautiful, sexy people looking beautiful and sexy in beautiful, sexy places – had been shoved in people's faces by the advertising and media industries since the 1920s, but as the millennium passed by, many came to the conclusion that it would never truly be theirs. They felt shut out, defrauded, excluded, humiliated and stranded on the outside looking in. All of this, and a good deal more besides, fomented the cynicism that is now such an important feature of contemporary life. It also laid the ground for the anger and resentment that lies at the core of the EDL. In the next chapter we look more closely at this political context.

TWO

Dead politics

It's the second week of May in 2015. The TV flashes and murmurs in the background as we write. The weird condensed melodrama of 24-hour news broadcasting is experiencing one of its gala events. Seeking but rarely finding an original and illuminating perspective, the usual pundits, publicists, bloggers and controversialists are queuing up to give the British people their hastily assembled take on the spectacular 2015 general election results. Contrary to the most informed predictions, the Conservatives have secured a small majority in the House of Commons.

In 2010 they had regained power after 13 painful years of opposition, but only with the support of the Liberal Democrats, which enabled the Conservatives to form the first coalition government in Britain since the end of the Second World War. It was not a resounding success for the Conservatives by any means, especially given that the outgoing Labour government had presided over the worst economic crisis in living memory. No matter. They were back and keen to get started.

Everyone agreed that the problems the Conservatives faced were significant. Since the crash of 2008, tax revenues had fallen precipitously, yet barely comprehensible amounts of money had been used to bail out 'too big to fail' banks. As the global financial system stalled, these banks found themselves on the verge of collapse and in desperate need of assistance from the state. By 2010 'tiny green shoots' of economic recovery had just begun to appear on the barren post-crash landscape, but the incoming coalition government continued to run a huge deficit. Indeed, this deficit seemed set to cast the British economy in shadow for the entirety of the coalition's term in office. As the outgoing Treasury Secretary Liam Byrne observed in a note left for his successor, there was, apparently, 'no money left' (Owen, 2010).

Members of the Conservative Party held the vast majority of the coalition's major cabinet posts. What first appeared to be a fragile coalition – composed of two political parties that possessed, on the surface of things, very different views on economic management, welfare and social justice – turned out to be remarkably strong. It was fully capable of coping with the choppy waters of parliamentary life to forge ahead with a radically cautious political programme couched in the language of apolitical pragmatism and ever-so-careful economic management. Commitment to cautious pragmatism within the stringent rules laid down by the hard-nosed accountancy that lies at the heart of neoliberal economics ensured that five years of unforgiving austerity followed the 2010 general election. The coalition government appeared resolute in its ambition to impose a measure of 'fiscal responsibility' on what it considered to be a sprawling, expensive and wasteful British public sector. The boom times were over and the country must cut its cloth accordingly.

From the outset the new government made it clear that the first order of business was to tackle the country's 'structural deficit'. This phrase was, at the time, a new addition to Westminster's obscure lingua franca. In the years that followed it would become commonplace. It referred not to debt but to a gaping hole in the government's finances that had grown significantly since the crisis of 2008. The money the country generated, mostly through taxation, was ominously less than the money it spent, mostly on the provision of services. Each year the government needed to borrow to fund its spending commitments, and each year, as the country's total debt grew, the deficit made it harder to pay it down. For many years following the Second World War Britain had run a budget surplus that justified high spending and fuelled the optimistic assumption that any high deficit would be paid off by increased industrial productivity. But the country had deindustrialised to become dependent on the financial and service sectors. Too little industry was left to grow and pay substantial wages and taxes.

The notably unimaginative and cautious nature of Westminster politics in the post-Blair era ensured that the only conceivable way to address this structural deficit was to reduce government spending. The old Keynesian principle of deficit spending – pumping money into the economy to improve infrastructure, increase demand and boost revenue-generating employment – had been dismissed by the neoliberal free-marketeers who had dominated both of Britain's major political parties since Labour's election victory in 1997. This situation was replicated throughout much of Europe and North America. Ultimately, austerity won the day unopposed. No alternative was offered to the British people, and there was a palpable absence of intelligent discussion of feasible alternative routes forward. Austerity was presented as a regrettable inevitability, even though many esteemed economists continued to warn of the perils of spending cuts during times of economic crisis (see, for example, Stiglitz, 2010; Keen, 2011; Varoufakis, 2011; Krugman, 2013).

There was no evidence to suggest that austerity would work, but plenty to suggest that it wouldn't. The rapid adoption of austerity policies across the west suggested a blind faith in the ideologies of the market. Despite the abandonment of idealism and the onward march of political pragmatism, there was little that was pragmatic, or indeed rational, about cutting back public spending in such an unremitting manner. Pragmatism is always blind to the fact that it is the servant of a disavowed ideal. Continuing austerity suggested that western political elites and their backroom advisers and experts were simply unwilling to relinquish their commitment to shrinking the state and encouraging profitable private enterprise. In the wake of the historic financial crisis of 2008, their retention of faith in the market appeared quite staggering. Everyone knew that austerity policies would hinder economic growth and push many into poverty, but austerity was asserted without doubt to be the only conceivable option.

Many on the political left argued that the budget cuts were too radical. However, it's worth exploring the possibility that the opposite was the case. Austerity policies were, in essence, not radical enough because they failed to address the fundamental causes of the financial crisis. Austerity represented a refusal to think imaginatively and competently about what needed to be done to secure the lifestyles of ordinary people, and it failed to take any action to prevent the repeat of the destructive financial conflagration of 2008. Given the evidence that suggested austerity would make matters worse rather than better, austerity appeared to be a kind of fetishistic self-flagellation imposed on the majority in order to guarantee that the super-rich minority were not inconvenienced too much, and could rest assured that with every passing year their wealth would continue to grow. The supposed pragmatism of austerity betrayed both the ideological and class commitments of those at the very top of our political system. Austerity appeared active and quite radical, but in reality this simply covered up a deeper inactivity. Politicians refused to address the fundamental issues at stake. Instead, they reasserted their faith in markets and busied themselves with activities that made matters worse.

Dealing with the deficit

In Britain, there was very little truly significant political debate on these issues. All the main political parties agreed that austerity was inevitable and the only feasible means of getting our economy back on an even keel. Rather than enter into a robust debate about the merits of austerity compared to other deficit-reduction strategies, Westminster limited its deliberations to the question of the speed at which unavoidable cuts were to be imposed. The differences between the main political parties were miniscule. The vast majority of mainstream politicians and elite media commentators who hung on to their every word accepted unconditionally that government spending must be cut, and that hard times lay ahead. Occasionally ministers seemed to have heavy hearts as they told voters that they were imposing cuts, but more often than not they argued that there was enough slack in the system to make the cuts without inconveniencing hard-working families or reducing frontline services.

The structural deficit was not the only problem Britain faced, but all of its other problems now seemed to relate to it in some way. Almost all state provision was to be either cut or scrapped altogether. Everything rested on accountants' abstract calculations of income, expenditure and 'value for money'. The real world of human experience seemed to be of secondary importance on the political agenda. For many watching events unfold on TV news broadcasts, every established entitlement that had once appeared fixed and dependable now seemed less so. What would be cut next, and how far would the cuts go?

The population was on average becoming progressively older. The money spent on pensions and care for the elderly had risen, and it was set to rise further still. Staggering sums of money were being spent on social welfare, even though mass unemployment was not a key outcome of the 2008 crisis in Britain. Given the state's difficult financial position, it was entirely predictable that a new campaign would arise to let hard-working taxpayers know that those revealed as 'spongers', 'malingerers' and 'skivers' would be the first to be penalised (see Tyler, 2013; Jensen and Tyler, 2015). Politicians in government spoke directly to those struggling to get by on low incomes. 'The problems you face personally, and the titanic economic problems we face together, are the result of welfare dependent skivers who want something for nothing. For too long governments of the left have indulged these skivers, but now we will tackle this problem so that hard-working families can again prosper.' And there it was. A historical crisis of capitalism, caused by the state's unwillingness to regulate the financial sector, by endemic short-termism and risk-taking in the city, and by a fundamental transformation in the hegemonic form of capital accumulation, had been ripped from its context, repackaged, and laid firmly at the door of the poorest and those with the least social and political power.

Almost all mainstream politicians seemed to agree that it was now time to reconsider the state's promise to its citizens. The polity and citizenry must now wake up and smell the coffee. A new day had dawned. If the economic problems that had descended on us were not tackled they would become progressively worse. It was better to nip potential disaster in the bud. Brave politicians must step forward, abandon the short-termism of the party political treadmill and, appealing to the masochistic guilt that seems to reside in the same dark cultural recess as our perverse Calvinist sense of fairness and just deserts, force the country to swallow the bitter medicine required to prevent catastrophe.

For those politicians firmly ensconced within the myopic and incestuous Westminster bubble, the reality of the country's grim situation appeared perfectly clear: the state could no longer afford to provide universal services in the way that it had done in the past. No one was prepared to admit that, as a replacement for the old productive economy, the British consumer-service economy had been an abject failure for many working people, who in reality had become nothing more than neoliberalism's collateral damage. With the plight of the real economy placed ideologically off-limits, the Conservative Party came into office promising to place the country on a firm fiscal and financial footing. They would impose unpopular policies, but they did so in the interests of all. Ossified and outdated bureaucracies had to be shaken from their slumber and forced to come to terms with a grim new reality in which every institution of government must be lean and efficient, ready to take on the challenges of delivering high quality public services as cheaply as possible. Stabilising the economy and pulling it out of the red were the priorities, and everything else trailed well behind.

'Small state' rhetoric had been reverberating around the halls of Westminster for decades. Classical economic liberalism's imperative to pull back the frontiers of the state had greatly influenced British politics before the crisis. This drive transformed the Conservative Party after Margaret Thatcher became party leader, and was integral to Tony Blair's 'modernisation' of the Labour Party. By 2008, when the crisis hit and its financial costs became clear, there were very few dissenting voices left in Parliament willing to challenge this narrative. Costs needed to be cut. The state needed to step back. The cost-efficient, waste-cutting private sector could fill the gaps, and encouraging it to do so would boost enterprise and reinvigorate the entrepreneurial spirit the country badly needed to prosper in such straitened times. Even though it was clear that the neoliberal model had fomented the crisis, there was still a general agreement that the free market, coaxed back to life by a briefly interventionist state, offered the best route back to sustained economic growth.

However, in setting out to revive the investment-profit-return cycle in this way, the state was, in effect, giving birth to its own eventual gravediggers. Once the state had nurtured the market back to health, representatives of the market would inevitably demand further privatisation, tax and spending cuts, and a reduction of its remit. Britain's political elite seemed to be reluctant to use the state in this way, but justified it to themselves and the population by agreeing that there was no other option. The purity of neoliberal theory needed to be set aside, and the market's representatives in government would have to countenance a brief flurry of state intervention. This intervention was very different to that of the post-war epoch. The state did not want to intervene, but felt forced to do so in the short term only so it could stop intervening in the longer term. This was no principled, long-term social democratic move to control profit-seeking and capital flight, re-invest capital or guarantee full employment. Once the market began to get moving, the neoliberal state would happily get the hell out of it and let the market continue on its merry way.

On the brink

It is important to remember the gravity of the financial crash, and just how close the British economy came to collapse. Unprecedented state intervention in the banking sector enabled the economy to overcome the initial shock, but a broad array of additional problems soon materialised. The shock of the crisis had sent markets into freefall. Surplus investment capital was languishing and depreciating in offshore accounts. The recklessness and risk-taking of the pre-crash years had been replaced by conservativism and risk-aversion. It was difficult for the investment class to find a sure thing to bet on. The dot.com bubble had burst and growth was slowing, even in the BRIC countries. Insecurity and doubt prevailed. The geopolitical situation was far from stable, and a number of sovereign states appeared to be on the verge of defaulting on their debts. Everywhere risks appeared magnified and financial markets remained jittery. In an attempt to calm those jitters, the state made it clear that it would stand shoulder to shoulder with the market. International financial institutions were also quick to use their huge economic power to restore confidence and steady the ship. Governments would do all they could to create a financially stable economic environment capable of encouraging the investment needed to get the market economy moving again.

The post-2008 free market was dependent on a financial type of state intervention unseen in human history. The state would need to counteract doubts and insecurities, and actively cultivate an environment in which the market economy could thrive. The markets needed an aggressively interventionist state to jump-start lending, and it was up to the state to recapitalise banks that found themselves exposed to a contagion of bad debt and worthless assets. State intervention of this kind runs contrary to free market theory, but government and the mass media played this down. Neoliberalism, during these years, was changing before our eyes. Academics would need to rethink the relationship between the state and the market, but all that was left for another day.

As the crisis unfolded it became increasingly clear that the wellbeing of the market was of the utmost importance to mainstream politicians of every stripe. Many politicians and academics were claiming that we had entered a strange post-ideological epoch that had forced on us a different kind of politics. Deep-seated ideological commitments had, apparently, been expunged from the political field, which was increasingly populated by grey bureaucrats immersed in pragmatic administrative tasks. Every day government, mainstream media and liberal academia instructed us to forget the great social antagonisms of the past. Class exploitation? What was that? Economically, 'we are all in it together' – 'it' being the market. Social antagonism was no longer economic but cultural. The identitarian antagonisms that had emerged during the 1960s and 1970s were rapidly pushed to the forefront of the popular imagination. The cultural interest groups that populated the arena of identity politics were promised incremental reformist solutions for 'inclusion' provided by the market's meritocratic and impartial social dynamism. In the new modish framework of 'intersectionality', class antagonism was either incorporated as just another social relation to take its place in the queue for attention, or dismissed as an unpalatable reminder of the world before progressive liberal multiculturalism.

However, the characteristics of this post-ideological era simply reflected the extinction of all alternatives to neoliberalism, and the transformation of neoliberalism itself into political and economic *doxa*, the common sense with which everyone was expected to agree. Once everyone had come to accept the rule of the market, there was no need for hostile ideological warfare, and no need for even passionate democratic engagement. The politics of the 21st-century's inaugural decade displayed a quite staggering degree of consensus on matters of political economy, even though our politicians disavowed this consensus and hyped up relatively trivial antagonisms in order to differentiate themselves. Ideological commitments had been discarded, their place taken by a commitment to careful pragmatic administration and growing the country's mainly service-based Gross Domestic Product (GDP). However, the pragmatic strategies adopted by mainstream politicians rested on a general ideological commitment to the market and the dominance of capital over everyday life. Once the market economy was fixed, the plethora of social problems that had arisen in recent years would gradually diminish.

In pursuit of this goal, right-wing liberals argued that the sovereign individual should be freed from state control, while left-wing liberals argued much the same, with the caveat that more should be done to include minority cultural groups and help the very poorest. In this monoculture of disavowed ideology, the entire sphere of politics appeared to lose much of its traditional substance. Influential liberals of the centre and the right agreed that the best way to accomplish their goals was to cut wasteful state services and encourage investment and private enterprise. Once something approaching stability had been restored, investment would pick up, unemployment would fall, tax revenues would rise, and once again all would be right with the world. Those a little further to the left argued that in the meantime offshore tax havens should be regulated and the mega-rich should be fairly taxed to maintain services. Every politician seemed to agree that everyone would benefit from a growing economy. The interests of employees and employers, the employed and the unemployed, the super-high-net-worth titans of Knightsbridge and the impoverished denizens of sink estates across the country appeared to converge on this issue. Market-led growth was the key, and the entirety of Westminster agreed that this mattered above all else.

This was not a genuine battle between left and right. No matter which political party you voted for, the result was pretty much the same. Great Britain's economic model had been set in stone, and all alternatives dismissed. Despite our deep immersion in an economic crisis that was driving up inequality and fomenting significant yet politically inarticulate and unrepresented anger among the people, no clash of ideologies took place on the field of politics (Winlow and Hall, 2012; Treadwell et al, 2013). Ideological commitment was signified as an anachronism, a deficit in critical thinking, an unhealthy liking for universal truths and an unwanted product of a disregard for the 'nuances and complexities' constantly uncovered by empirical evidence. Those who believed wholeheartedly in a specific social and political model were dismissed as blinkered and unable to appreciate the benefits of adopting a pick-and-mix pluralistic approach to the realm of ideas.

Across the political spectrum most seemed to agree that every strategy geared towards boosting investment and shoring up profits should be placed on the table ready to be deployed by the pragmatists in government and the apparatchiks that pulled the strings in our global financial institutions. Ideology, they said, had nothing to do with it. This was not a time to listen to the wittering of unworldly cloistered intellectuals. Action needed to be taken right now to hold together the basic economic foundations of western civilisation. The basic principles of Keynesianism and the archaic tracts of market fundamentalism would be of little use in addressing problems of such staggering magnitude. To restore equilibrium the state must be willing to debt-generate barely fathomable amounts of capital as quantitative easing to shore up failing banks. This strange hybrid strategy, that used state intervention to secure the circulation of capital, was certainly not Keynesian demand management in the traditional sense, but neither was it neoclassicism. Mindful of the loss of faith in the market after the Great Depression and the Second World War, the goal was to return the freshly tainted market system to the position of supremacy it was destined to occupy as quickly as possible. And to do that they were willing to stray far from established market principles – but only as a temporary measure.

If this was pragmatism, it was pragmatism with a view to recreating the idealised pre-crash order, with all its inherent flaws and injustices. In essence this is no different to the EDL's yearning for an idealised industrial social democratic past in which their class, communities and culture seemed secure, and no different to radical Islam's own return to fundamentals. In the absence of an alternative future, all seek their own retrogressive escape route from the neoliberal market's unforgiving insecurity. The globalised marketplace was king and the state was its servant. No serviceable and appealing alternative existed. The hypnotic allure of high investment returns and rapidly rising property values, just like the good old days, drew politicians back to the dogma of markets like moths to a flame. After all, what does success look like for the career politicians of Westminster? How will they be judged by history? How they respond to external threats such as terrorism is important, but the real test for Britain's 21st-century political leaders would be the economy.

Money, wealth and libidinous enjoyment had supplanted the grand transcendental ideals of the modern age: equality, freedom, solidarity, justice. What were these abstractions when compared to the earthy reality of economic performance and its hedonistic rewards? People talked of their commitment to these ideals, but underneath it all only money and prosperity really mattered. Everyone from the corporate executive to the careerist academic to the mobile working-class entrepreneur wanted more of it. It was the way of the world. Consumer culture had eroded a broad range of cultural values to the extent that access to more and better consumer goods and 'safe spaces' in which to consume them had become a primary social end desired by all, a prize our politicians would bestow on us if they were successful in boosting investment and economic growth. As our identikit politicians rolled off the Westminster production line in red, blue or yellow ties, they had this phrase drummed into them:

above all else, make the majority feel richer and safer. Electorally insignificant, the very poorest simply did not matter.

Because the state had placed itself fully at the disposal of the market – bailing out private banks with its unprecedented quantitative easing programme and reducing interest rates to historic lows – it somehow needed to boost its income and reduce its outgoings. It seemed natural for the state to divest itself of assets that accrued a cost. These assets could be sold off to provide the government with a much-needed cash injection. In the very same movement the private sector would be invigorated and provided with new opportunities for profit, and the general public would, in all likelihood, benefit as consumer and leisure options expanded. In a country that had discarded labour-intensive and export-orientated industry, the service industry was the primary investment target. Many of those services that remained in the public sector were sold off or contracted out. The rationale for this was very much the same. The profit motive would help the various business entities involved in the provision of formerly public services to identify waste, cut costs and bring efficiency to an outdated and sclerotic welfare state (see, for example, Whitehead and Crawshaw, 2013; Whitehead, 2015). The profit motive would ensure that standards were kept high while costs were cut to the bone. In these hard times, the lethargy and inefficiency thought to be inevitable by-products of state bureaucracy could no longer be tolerated.

The outcomes of those five years of Tory-led coalition government are now quite clear. The gap between rich and poor continued to grow to proportions not seen since the Victorian era. The welfare state was further stripped back and sold off (Mendoza, 2015). The social fabric of Britain deteriorated, and competitive individualism solidified its position at the core of our culture (Winlow and Hall, 2013; Raymen, 2015; Smith and Raymen, 2015). A great diversity of social problems worsened at alarming rates (O'Hara, 2015). The majority displayed progressively less empathy for those who found themselves impoverished, sick or otherwise at the margins of British society (Tyler, 2013). The logic of the market economy achieved a fully doxic position as the timeless and immutable common sense to which all mainstream politicians must subscribe (Varoufakis,

2013). Over the coalition's five years in office, simmering anger and dissatisfaction were stoked up further by the growing gap between ordinary people – facing diminished job prospects, falling incomes and reduced state services – and the professional politicians of Westminster who refused to budge from their commitment to the free market.

The Liberal Democrats' performance in the 2010 election was, at the time, quite startling; it seemed that many disillusioned Labour and Conservative voters had switched their allegiance in the belief that the party could effect real change and bring some much needed moral energy and ideological contestation to Britain's ailing two-party system. However, after five years in coalition government, it became clear that the Lib Dems were simply a small party committed to the same orthodoxies as the Conservative and Labour Parties. The Lib Dems possessed no real dynamism and offered no real alternative. When chances presented themselves they failed to challenge the political and economic conventions of the day. They had not spoken up for those most in need of a vocal and steadfast advocate. As the general shape and trajectory of the 2010-15 coalition became clear, yet another putative alternative revealed itself to be a sham, and support for the Lib Dems sharply fell away.

The magic money tree

It is important to keep in mind that the true causes of the 2008 economic crash – which will continue to shape our economies for many years to come – cannot be reduced to the tendency of left-of-centre governments to spend beyond their means. The success of the narrative that accuses Blairite 'third way' governments of irresponsibly lavish spending binges during the boom times, leaving the governments that followed to pick up the tab, has been truly remarkable. It has been repeated so often by politicians and media pundits that it has encouraged many to conclude that it must be true. The narrative benefits from a folksy wisdom: it seems to make sense because its central issues have been reconfigured to fit in with common experience. The average household in Britain now carries somewhere in the region of £10,000 in unsecured debts – mostly overdrafts, personal loans and credit card debts (Press Association, 2015; see also Horsley, 2015 for a detailed analysis) — so it is easy to see why so many ordinary people were able to construct an analogy between national and household economics as the basis for understanding and believing this account of the cause of the crisis. It is, of course, quite absurd to suggest that national debt is even remotely similar to household debt. Unlike households struggling to pay debts, sovereign nations have the capacity to validate and print their own currency, tax imports and so on. The Bank of England also has the ability to set interest rates and control the money supply. Quite clearly, the debts faced by sovereign nations are entirely different to those faced by households. But we must recognise that this narrative achieves primacy precisely because all mainstream politicians and mass media controllers have bought into it.

Even the current crop of Labour politicians, many of whom were in government when news of the crisis first broke, admit that mistakes were made. With hindsight, they should have perhaps pulled back on spending to level out the boom, banking the money safely so it could be drawn on when the hard times returned. Many politicians on the left blamed decadent risk-taking individuals for the crisis, or the inaction of back office regulators in the banks, or the greed that has become so integral to the culture of the investment banking industry. However, they offered only a moral critique of the anti-social rich when what was necessary was an objective analysis of the huge risks associated with abstract financial markets as they tried to come to terms with permanent low growth and surplus capital in a world of declining resources and saturated consumer markets. Once we understand that capitalism is energised solely by individuals seeking their own economic best interests, and that it actively cultivates forms of social life and subjectivity that revel in competition and personal achievement calibrated against the downfall of 'losers', we can begin to see that moral critique is of little use to us. In the build-up to the 2008 crash, the investment banking industry's front office risk-takers, aided by the middle office 'quants' who design rickety high-risk financial instruments, were simply doing what they were supposed to be doing. Corporations exist to make a profit. Everything they do is orientated to this end.

The high-profile front office denizens of the investment banking industry are not 'geniuses' but simply salespeople with a knack for identifying profitable investment opportunities and convincing investors to invest. They thrive on risk-taking, competition and one-upmanship, and, of course, they tend to be attuned to the dog-eat-dog world of high finance. They are unadorned liberals in the classical sense: they believe absolutely that individuals act in relation to their own perceived economic best interests. To argue that this group of people – all of whom had the profit-at-all-costs ethos drummed into them during their corporate socialisation – should have withdrawn from opportunities to turn a profit and focused instead on the wellbeing of others, and the overall integrity of the global financial markets, is sheer wishful thinking. Throwing out the bad capitalists and replacing them with good capitalists is not an option, because the moment a capitalist abandons economic self-interest he is no longer a capitalist.

Only a few of those outside democratic politics – mainly marginal academics, campaigners and political activists – were capable of identifying market capitalism itself as the ultimate issue at stake. However, these outsiders were simply denied a voice in mainstream politics, media and academia. Thus they were denied the opportunity to broadcast truths about the capitalist market, its founding principle of unequal exchange and its inherent tendency towards reckless and amoral profit-seeking and chronic instability. Therefore the people could not be brought into an encounter with the fundamental causes of the crisis. The long-running evolution of capitalism and the rise of abstract financial speculation and trading were barely discussed beyond the university campus. There was little mention of the growing gap between the abstract financial markets and the real economy that produces useful goods, and in which ordinary people find their work, livelihoods and security. When it was mentioned, it was done in measured terms and framed as a problem to be solved by boosting the sort of regulation and taxation that investment bankers are expert at avoiding.

It seemed impossible to go much further than this. The spectrum of British politics had changed so much that even to propose modest forms of social democratic intervention – perhaps beginning with a national investment bank, the renationalisation of key industries and services such as energy and the railways, and a concerted attempt to raise tax revenues from corporations and the super-rich – were represented as illiberal, even the slippery slope to communist totalitarianism. What between 1945 and 1979 had been a centrist economic orthodoxy to which both political parties adhered was dismissed out of hand. All who advocated such measures were unceremoniously catapulted to the margins of politics, academia and mass-mediated culture. The metropolitan elite who had seized control of British politics, media and much of the education and research system remained utterly dedicated to the continuity of free-market capitalism. The liberals of the Labour Party had, they believed, learned the economic lessons of the 1970s and the political lessons of the 1980s. They had learned to appreciate Hayek, Friedman and the benefits of the free market, and they had learned that above all the voters of middle England wanted personal prosperity and the promise of upward mobility.

Mainstream politicians across the political spectrum argued constantly that the staggering wealth of the super-rich benefited all. Those who suggest otherwise simply revealed themselves to be envious losers opposed to individual economic freedom. Those who maintained a commitment to the principles of social democracy and recoiled at the anti-social and environmentally destructive tendencies of unabashed neoliberalism were now derided as commies, Trotskyites, the traitorous enemy within. For those at the centre, it all seemed so obvious: the rich were not the enemy. Those who continued to portray the rich in this way were simply relics from the past. It was clear to anyone with a brain that without the risk-taking and boundless ingenuity of the new corporate elite we would all be destitute, and our economy would be in ruins. If the free market remained free and those who populate it were allowed to go about their business unimpeded we would all *eventually* see our standards of living improve.

It was not simply that the leading lights of New Labour grudgingly went along with this; rather, they were active, card-carrying advocates of the free market. For 13 years under Tony Blair and Gordon Brown they had been in the driving seat, during which time they did much to advance this agenda. Inequality grew. Brown, in particular, argued strongly for the benefits of light-touch regulation and the free movement of capital. By this time New Labour was no longer really a socialist or even a social democratic party in the proper sense. Indeed, the Blairite party elite were no longer dedicated to advancing the interests of labour. The Parliamentary Labour Party (PLP) had stylishly sashayed, Pinot Grigio in hand, across the political spectrum to occupy ground traditionally associated with the political right. Once there they blithely rewrote history, claiming that this had always been the Labour Party's natural uncontested position. This ground was rightfully theirs.

Ideologically, though, the move was shrouded in fetishistic disavowal, a psychological technique that allows the individual to choose to systematically repress and ultimately forget truth. The individual can disavow knowledge of that which is upsetting, injurious or sensitive by pushing it from consciousness into the unconscious. In this case, the good neoclassical liberals of New Labour were able to strip their own cynical revisionist political activity of all negative connotations and repackage it as a good and necessary thing. They set out to convince themselves and others that they were still dedicated to their traditional task of improving the conditions of working people throughout an increasingly classless society, and their bone-crushingly obvious move to the right had not been a move to the right at all. They had simply recognised that some of the old commitments of the Labour Party needed to change.

New Labour looked out upon what it saw as a totally transformed political and economic vista. The rabble-rousing of the past was counterproductive. The interests of workers were now to be advanced in tandem with the interests of employers, investors and shareholders. Working men and women did better when hedge-fund managers, sprawling corporations and the new global super-rich did better. At some point the wealth would all trickle down. The time for class conflict was over. Indeed, all talk of social class was silenced. It was all rather unseemly, totally outdated and ultimately useless in helping Britain adapt to the remorseless competition of the new global marketplace. Instead, New Labour concerned itself primarily with those who aspired, with its bleeding heart reserved solely for those who could be expediently defined as the 'deserving poor'. Its great endeavour was to turn Britain into a meritocracy, but little consideration was given to the able-bodied who failed to display the social ambition and upgraded occupational skills that would ensure their own upward mobility.

It is worth reminding ourselves that meritocracy was a concept created in jest. It was never supposed to be taken seriously. Nevertheless, the joke did not seem to register with the new generation of party apparatchiks that allocating resources to those who possessed 'talent' – a quality squeezed into one dimension, hardened and impoverished by the demands of the marketplace – was scarcely more just than allocating resources on the basis of one's family bloodline. By this time the cult of the entrepreneur, constantly shoved in the population's face by mass media and politicians alike to the extent that some became TV celebrities, had transformed our values and popular culture to a mode in which being 'talented' had become synonymous with advancing one's own personal interests by means of sharp business dealing. Alternative sources of value had been sucked into the money nexus. 'Talent' translated exclusively into business and wealth, and it was business and wealth that really mattered.

The Labour Party's commitment to equality gradually morphed into a commitment to 'equality of opportunity'. New Labour could now focus on enabling hard-working and talented members of the lower orders to set about the task of transforming their lives and their circumstances. This is how we were to beat inequality. Little thought was given to the majority who failed, for whatever reason, to win out in the competitive struggle for personal success and got left behind. Still, New Labour now held a special place in its heart for those who strived. The term 'striver' entered the popular lexicon. New Labour's long-standing commitment to common ownership was discarded. Generally, New Labour swam with the tide and accepted the triumph of individualism over old-fashioned ideas rooted in collectivism and solidarity.

By the time Tony Blair was ousted from political power, his brand sullied by illegal invasions, widening social inequality and constant kowtowing to the United States of America, the majority of the PLP were dedicated neoliberals, true believers in the benefits of the free market and its growing army of entrepreneurs. However, one or two characteristics still separated them from their brethren in blue on the other side of the debating chamber. Some of New Labour's neoliberals still retained a degree of guilt about their neoliberalism, and that guilt encouraged the adoption of a philanthropic attitude toward the disadvantaged, which occasionally leaked over the boundary separating the 'deserving' from the 'non-deserving'. They had not yet fully hardened themselves to the suffering of others, and were not yet convinced by the voluntarist doctrine that the poor brought all their problems upon themselves.

Had they been a little more honest with themselves, New Labour's slightly guiltier neoliberals would have admitted that they had uncritically adopted too much of Thatcher's market deification and anti-social dogma. They had blindly rushed after a Conservative Party, itself undergoing its own significant changes, in the hope of appealing to a small number of swing voters in marginal seats who appeared capable of pushing election results one way or the other. The working-class grassroots of the party were treated with disdain, and the solid Labour seats in Scotland, Wales and the North of England were forgotten. New Labour's rush for the centre ground drew its attention away from the fact that since 1979 the centre of the British political spectrum had been moving to the right. They threw off their ill-fitting, old-fashioned workerist garb and clad themselves in the trendy new attire of individualism, achievement, freedom and competition. The PLP became aloof and unconcerned about the things that mattered to the men and women who populated their constituencies and continued to vote Labour in the absence of a more appealing alternative. Traditional Labour voters were taken for granted. The PLP was convinced that, no matter what, these voters could never bring themselves to vote for the Conservatives. Thus the PLP felt confident that adopting policies likely to appeal to swing voters was the best strategy in the fight to secure office. The working class in the former industrial heartlands, decaying inner cities and excised semi-rural settlements could be forgotten. The focus should be on undecided voters in middle England, voters with no traditional class allegiance to either of the main political parties; voters who could, at a push, when conditions were temporarily conducive, be persuaded to vote New Labour instead of Conservative.

As time passed it became increasingly obvious to all that New Labour had become totally disconnected from the core principles on which the original Labour Party was founded. It was not a party of the working class or those who aspired towards social justice, and it was no longer a party that guaranteed economic participation and redistribution of wealth. The PLP had cut itself adrift from its own political and cultural history to fulfil its desperate yearning to win office. It had followed Thatcher and Blair in meekly accepting the stringent rule of the market over everyday life. The rough-hewn labour politics of the past were forgotten. The party's roots in the trade union movement were forgotten. The party's commitment to redistribution and social justice were forgotten. The party had been taken over by liberals, and these liberals were sure that the party was theirs by right, a sentiment evidenced quite recently by the upper-class Blairite MP Tristram Hunt's recent appeal to the Oxbridge elite to re-establish control of a Labour Party dumped 'in the shit' by the election of Jeremy Corbyn as leader (Perraudin, 2015). Anyone who spoke of traditional commitments was shouted down and dismissed as a pound-shop Trot, an anachronism, a splitter, an electoral liability who should be unceremoniously kicked out.

This process was aided by the active recruitment of intellectually undercooked PPE graduates, Blairite marketeers and third way social administration functionaries principally concerned with forging lucrative careers as professional politicians. However, even these entryist apparatchiks, most of whom had little knowledge of the pressures faced in the real world by ordinary men and women, were still keen to distinguish themselves from the Tories. Following Blair, they remained dedicated to the market and the reallocation of resources upwards, but they hoped to convince voters that they were marginally less beastly than the Tories. They would agree with the Tories on economic issues, but sought to distinguish themselves by, on the surface of things, defending the welfare state and funding a range of measures to help the poorest. For the Blairites – convinced that neoliberal capitalism creates a rising tide that lifts all boats rather than a tsunami that swamps all but the biggest – all social groups thrive in a growing economy. This, in turn, meant that every effort must be made to ensure that business leaders were freed from the burdens of regulation and taxation so that they could drive economic growth through innovation and investment. For New Labour, the gap between rich and poor mattered little as long as both groups did better in economic terms.

Freedom for the wealth creators

Central to Blair's 'third way' was the belief that freeing the 'wealth creators' from state intervention would drive economic growth, and as a consequence of this, more tax money would flow into the coffers of the exchequer. This money could then be used to attend to some of the more pressing needs of the poorest. However, after the crash it became increasingly obvious that, in an effectively borderless global economy in which technological innovation enabled money to traverse the world instantaneously, the nation-state was entirely incapable of ensuring that corporations and the new super-rich paid what they owed. The tax avoidance industry was by this time pervasive, complex and highly advanced in its methods. Corporations were increasingly savvy to the benefits of offshoring taxable income in competitor states where corporate tax rates were lower. Money earned in the UK by big-name corporations could be registered as income in offshore tax havens. Money that could have been used to address welfare funding or the structural deficit was simply claimed and retained as temporarily dormant surplus capital waiting for the next high-return investment opportunity anywhere in the world. The general reluctance to address this problem ensured an unseemly race to the bottom. States transformed themselves into 'economic actors' and competed against neighbouring states to lower corporate tax as much as need be to attract corporations and super-rich individuals onto their territory. Of course, for corporations this was a win–win situation. A detailed analysis carried out in 2012 suggested that between £13 trillion and £20 trillion has been hidden away in the offshore banking system (see Stewart, 2012; see also Shaxson, 2012).

Neoliberalism is, of course, extremist, and the problems it causes are extreme, but this demonic label is reserved exclusively for any substantive opposition. The 'far left' – that is, the left that proposes to build a new socioeconomic system on a firm commitment to equality and social justice – was, of course, locked out of popular debates about the crisis. Those 'extremist' elements of leftist politics that remain committed to moving beyond global capitalism were dismissed as simply beyond the pale. An unpalatable reminder of the class antagonisms of the 20th century, they had committed the cardinal sin of failing to move with the times. The politicians and media commentators who occupied the mainstream placed the radical left who talked of equality and social justice in the same category of retrograde extremism as the radical right who talked of racial purity and the defence of the homeland, or the Stalinists who in another era sent dissenters to the Gulags. Only atavistic ideologues intoxicated by the prospect of imposing their rigid ideological blueprints on an inherently pluralistic social world populated by freedom–loving individuals exercising their inalienable right to enrich themselves would ever dream of dispensing with the productive and organisational wonders brought to us by new 'creative' markets and driven forward by the profit motive. Even during times of global economic crisis, and right across the spectrum of mainstream western politics, there remained a steadfast commitment to the by-now mythical 'free market'.

However, as we have seen, neoliberalism's idealised 'free market' is in reality an unstable, crisis–ridden state- and taxpayer-funded chimera that is yet to deliver the steady economic growth of the regulated post-war social democratic years. The growth that has occurred since the rise of global neoliberalism has been patchy to say the least. Nevertheless, despite the rise of oppositional groups like Occupy, and despite a growing awareness of proliferating harms and injustices, global neoliberal capitalism is still the only game in town. People across the west structure their ambitions, dreams and desires in relation to it. Every imaginable alternative political and economic system seems immeasurably worse by comparison. Capitalism had, most people believed, delivered to us untold riches and an unprecedented material quality of life. It had driven forward scientific discovery and filled our world with technological wizardry and the sensuous delights of consumerism (see Miles, 2015). Marx's 19th-century capitalism, based on the brutal expropriation of surplus value created by workers, has been superseded. To reinforce the system's ideological framework the compulsory celebration of capitalism's benefits, orchestrated by the dominant political and media class, encouraged a relativistic acceptance of the system's hugely problematic undercurrents and outcomes.

Even though a cursory inspection of Britain's employment practices and working environments might suggest that early capitalism's tendency to brutal exploitation had been overcome, western corporations had, like taxable income, offshored their sweatshops and satanic mills. Neoliberalism has not fostered a culture of *denial*, as Cohen's (2000) outdated thesis suggests, but a culture of *acceptance* among the everyday population. Our political and cultural leaders are also quite willing to take the risk of publicly admitting that brutal exploitation and harm of the capitalist kind can now be found in the developing world, where workers toil in dangerous conditions for incredibly low rates of pay in order to ensure that westerners are able to access relatively cheap consumer items. Things were bad, there was no denial of that, but our leaders stressed that even in the most impoverished areas things were improving. Even those working in brutal and insecure conditions in the developing world are no longer starving, and even in those areas where people continue to starve, they are no longer starving in the numbers they once had been. Thus we should accept the way things are because as long as nations comply with neoliberal logic, these things are not fixed and continue to improve. Eventually, capitalism and the magic of the market will deliver us from evil.

However, the sentiments expressed by supporters of the EDL later in this book suggest quite clearly that, as far as they are concerned, in the reality outside the unending neoliberal pep talk that dominates politics and the mass communications system, the democratic system in Britain has failed. This reality is founded on a simple economic anomaly characteristic of advanced global capitalism – returns on capital are greater than growth in the real productive economy (Piketty, 2014). Labour-intensive production centres are therefore viable only in regions of cheap labour, land, materials and taxes. Now into their third generation, the inhabitants of the old English industrial regions can sense their own historical redundancy, and regard as an incontrovertible fact their grounded perception that their former champions and protectors, the Labour Party and the liberal left in general, have nothing of any substance to offer them. To these discarded workers the metropolitan middle class's posturing hipster communism and shrill identity politics is particularly galling. Thus eyes turn to the right, and the far right appears on the radar screen as the only alternative option.

The rise of UKIP

In the early years of the 21st century UKIP drew a great deal of support precisely because it sought to challenge the dominance of the Labour and Conservative parties. The dourness of the political scene, with its stage-managed theatrics, interminable fudging and meaningless blathering on, had prompted the electorate to lose interest and grow cynical, but here was a political party that hoped to challenge and depose the dominant Westminster orthodoxy.

UKIP had originally been a left-of-centre Eurosceptic party, founded in 1991 by the London School of Economics (LSE) historian and former liberal Alan Sked, but it rapidly shifted across the political spectrum as it learned to move beyond mere Euroscepticism to play on traditional concerns about nationhood, culture and the threats posed by immigrants. These were issues of great importance to many, but vigilantly avoided by the major political parties, or else their representatives spouted vacuous platitudes in the hope of sounding statesmanlike and multicultural, while at the same time being so consummately vague that no one could be either soothed or angered by what had been said. The number of immigrants coming in to the country had risen substantially, and many living in working-class neighbourhoods were keenly aware of this significant change and anxious about the future.

Unable to locate and understand the objective source of their fear in the recent convulsions of the global capitalist system, and working in the intellectual darkness created by its ideologues of right and left, UKIP helped them to reach the conclusion that the rapid arrival of large numbers of immigrants was disrupting their community life and diluting their culture. They felt that their chances of finding and keeping a reasonably remunerative job were declining as new economic competitors made their way to the UK to undercut wages and work competitively long hours. Tired of following the Calvinist command to blame themselves for their loss of work and status, and unable to blame capitalism's abstract system, once again they identified a scapegoat. There was little cultural 'Othering' associated with this – UKIP had officially confirmed their suspicion that a concrete threat had moved into their territory, and, once again, they believed. At last, it seemed that a political party had come into being that was willing to defy convention and talk honestly about an issue of genuine importance. While the party has a leafy Home Counties feel to it and its leader Nigel Farage was formerly a finance industry denizen, the overwhelming majority of its support in the 2015 election came from the white working class.

Farage set out to cultivate a 'man of the people' demeanour. He was remarkably successful. He quickly drew support because at the time he seemed quite different from the vacuous identikit politicians who dominated Westminster. He spoke openly and in a manner which suggested that his responses were unscripted. He appeared in innumerable photos drinking beer and smoking cigarettes. Here, it seemed, was a man we could all relate to: devoid of airs and graces, a man who enjoyed a drink and talked knowledgeably and passionately about immigration and its effects. Perhaps more to the point, he showed disdain for the political conventions of the day, and set himself apart from Westminster's shallow, presentational political correctness.

When attacked and labelled a racist, Farage responded by suggesting that he was only raising issues that were of genuine importance to everyday people. There was, he said, nothing inherently racist about arguing for tougher immigration controls.

He also spoke with great commitment about the need to defend British jobs and the threat posed by unchecked immigration to the nation's culture and heritage. He talked of reaffirming British sovereignty and withdrawing from the European Union (EU). For him, Britain's involvement in the EU meant that billions of pounds were being wasted on pointless bureaucracy. Policies that harmed Britain were being forced on the country by grey bureaucrats who cared little about the problems faced by ordinary men and women. He said that ordinary people would be immeasurably better off if the country shifted course and withdrew from the EU. It was a broadly felt desire for palpable change that allowed UKIP to grow so quickly into a genuine force in British politics.

However, the rise of UKIP must be placed in an appropriate context. It would be entirely wrong to dismiss UKIP voters as stupid racists who draw sustenance purely from the ideologies of historical imperialism and 20th-century nationalism. In the absence of any other mode of understanding, UKIP's anti-immigration policies often seem quite logical and attractive to those members of the white working class who remain very anxious about their jobs and status. From their point of view, as we will see, more migrants simply mean more competition for jobs, security and status. For many voters the threats posed by mass immigration are quite clear. If immigration is allowed to continue at current levels, they believe, it will become progressively harder to get and keep a job, and increased competition will suppress wage levels. UKIP's drive to close the UK's borders might seem a rather basic strategy if the goal is to secure the economic security of the nation, but to many white working-class voters this seemed like a perfectly reasonable and entirely necessary practical move, and one likely to deliver immediate success.

Beneath Farage's raffishness and UKIP's headline-grabbing anti-EU and anti-immigration policies lies a highly conventional commitment to the free market. On the surface of things, UKIP appears to be defying convention, but if we look a little deeper, it becomes obvious that it is, in fact, a populist right-wing party committed to lowering taxes, shrinking the state and reinvigorating British business. Understandably enough, we hear a great deal about UKIP's desire to close the nation's borders to immigrants and its desire to drag the nation clear of the structural ineptitude of the EU, but little has been said about its approach to economic management. UKIP has itself remained quite vague about these issues, and few detailed policy suggestions have been placed before the British people. However, judging by those policy suggestions made available, it seems that UKIP hopes to drive new forms of competition and create in Britain a more dynamic market for capital accumulation. It also hopes to significantly reduce taxation and shrink still further current welfare provision. Of course, these issues often appear to escape the attention of working-class voters attracted by UKIP's swashbuckling anti-Westminster rhetoric and its promise to reduce immigration. Should we assume that, when working-class voters vote for UKIP, we are witnessing yet another instance of the poorest voting against their class interests? If so, the absence of a true alternative in popular culture looks to be backfiring more dangerously than anyone imagined – so dangerous is this political turn, in fact, that the liberal left and the Labour Party might never dare admit the crucial part they played in it.

What ex-working-class voters would get with a UKIP government is hard-core Thatcherism, perhaps with a nastier Randian edge to it, tougher immigration policies, withdrawal from the EU, closer ties with corporate USA, and greater susceptibility to the strategies of the global finance industry. UKIP accepts the ultimate horizon of neoliberal economic management. However, its desire to defend British business appears slightly confused. Is it really possible to commit to the free market while at the same time defending the interests of British business and labour? Are the interests of British business best served by withdrawal from the EU, which is Britain's primary export market? And given the dispersed and shifting ownership of most large corporations, is it even possible to talk of 'British business' in the same way we could in years gone by? Isn't there a fundamental antagonism in advocating economic freedom and the free movement of capital yet seeking to restrict the free movement of workers across borders? Ultimately, it seems, UKIP wants to have its cake and eat it. It wants to retain the best bits of the market economy while discarding what it considers the negative outcomes of 21st-century neoliberalism. UKIP's economic policies are, of course, deemed relatively unimportant because it joins the larger political parties of Westminster in accepting absolutely the core principles of market economies. Of far more interest to the voting public is UKIP's cultural message, some of which is out there in the open, and some of which is hidden and implied. This crucial distinction reflects a deeper and more fundamental schism that has appeared in the political realm: on the one hand, the unchallengeable supremacy of the free market, and on the other, a shift towards rather basic, two-dimensional 'cultural' relations as the principal sphere of social antagonism.

THREE

The fickle parent

While traditional nationalism transcends class, the vast majority of our EDL contacts are from the old Labour heartlands, the former industrial working-class regions once feared by the establishment as seedbeds of socialism. Although most have been disengaged from the political system for a very long time, a significant number acknowledged a familial connection to the Labour Party or the trade union movement. Their parents or grandparents tended to be Labour voters, and some of our key contacts talked in detail about the involvement of their fathers in once powerful trade unions that won significant concessions from industry bosses and advanced the lifestyles of working men and women substantially during the middle third of the 20th century. It would be wrong to assume that most of these men were once working-class Tories.

From where we sit as academics, on our comfortable ledge as surplus wage workers in the educational bureaucracy, reasonably well paid to do little more than reproduce a humanitarian worldview by levering its carefully selected cultural issues and approved post-political solutions to the top of the agenda, 'the left' might appear to be alive and in rude health. Enriched and enlivened by its new focus on cultural diversity rather than the dour and intractable neoliberal economy, to some it might even appear stronger than ever, about to regroup itself into a truly potent force and once more become the agent of history. However, for many of the old working class, especially those who occupy the old Labour heartlands, 'the left' today is totally irrelevant. It can no longer effect real change, and it can no longer be considered a substantive force in the world. It appears only as an optical illusion visible from all angles but their own, like an image on an old lenticular novelty card.

Before the left disappeared from the residual group's perspective, it would seem that, generally speaking, at a fundamental level the English middle class and working class understood it as two very different things. A minority of the waged workers who identified with the old working class and belonged to its various communities for generations were socialists or communists, but the majority belonged to two main groups. One group saw the institutionalised Labourite left as a guardian that would protect and sustain their hard-won economic foothold on the industrial capitalist order and the passably stable rhythms of life that had slowly evolved in their communities. The other group put their faith in the establishment, represented for most by Labour's right wing, for reasons that ranged from anti-communist ideology to a keen appreciation of the logical link between profitable business and the continuation of their own jobs. However, both were bound together by the common principle of continuity and stability, the attainment of which, some thought, occasionally required the paradox of militant politics. In true and schismatic contradistinction, however, the liberal middle class, whose historical suspicion of the working-class left seemed to have been confirmed once and for all by the brutal totalitarian outcomes of revolutionary politics in the 20th century, saw the left as worthy of existence only on their own terms, as an agent of the relentless cultural subversion and transformation that they thought would lead to freedom of lifestyle for individuals, and the equalisation of rights and economic opportunities for the diverse gender and ethnic groups it claimed to represent.

This process of subversion and transformation – no bad thing if it could be equally beneficial – was to be set in motion without any fundamental restructuring of capitalism's polarised class relation or intervention in its deep economic and cultural logics, which, respectively, are founded on profitability and competitive individualism. This task has now been passed across from the old, dying institutionalised left to the 'leaderless multitude', to be undertaken in a way yet to be decided over an indeterminate period of time. Truth to tell, in the neoliberal period the new middle-class left – deeply afraid of the return of past totalitarian

46

horrors and intoxicated by visions of a future filled with unprecedented liberties delivered to us by a capitalist system that they would make more just and democratic on everyone's behalf – moved further away from the traditional working-class left than the old conservative right had ever been. Some on the new cultural left still held hope in Marx's yearning that the new world would dissolve both antagonistic classes, yet they were also quite sanguine or perhaps even relieved that the proletariat would have to go first.

On the other side of the fence the neoliberal right has been proclaiming the left's death since Margaret Thatcher's ascent to power. Indeed, they are happy to take the credit for it. However, the reality is far more disturbing. Ashamed of the past atrocities committed in its name and worried about its professional survival in a liberal-capitalist world it now thought could no longer be changed, the traditional communist and socialist left seemed to disappear into thin air in the 1960s. Some of its former advocates returned quickly to the metropolitan political scene, reincarnated as the cultural 'new left'. At the same time, tired of trying to maintain its transcendental ideals and hold back the tide of social and cultural change, the traditional Christian conservative right meekly accepted the new role allocated to it by the triumphant neoliberals – to work in the background maintaining a semblance of the old moral order that might attenuate the worst excesses of the neoliberal economic experiment. Neither the bold communists nor the traditional moralists could beat the neoliberal system. Therefore, for the more ambitious individuals from these two groups, it seemed like the only option was to join it.

As the historical class struggle subsided and the two old political adversaries disintegrated, the centrist factions consolidated their positions in the new bio-political administrative system that was to replace the old antagonistic class politics and the older intersecting cultural struggle between conservative traditionalism and liberal progressivism. By the 1990s, after the fall of the Soviet Union and the decline of the west's Christian moral majority, the combined forces of neoliberal capitalism and liberal culturalism triumphed over socialism and conservatism in all spheres – politics, economics and culture. We were told by established liberal intellectuals that we had entered the era of allegedly new 'third way' conciliatory politics at the end of history. It was difficult to recognise too many substantive differences between this and old-school social liberalism, but the shiny new logo gave pundits something to write about. The enduring triumph of capitalism and liberalism was proclaimed from the liberal left by the likes of Anthony Giddens and from the liberal right by the likes of Francis Fukuyama.

We could aver that their willingness to articulate this historical victory for popular consumption was the primary reason why these two intellectuals and their fellow luminaries became established in the first place. For politicians, academics and media functionaries this was the new way to be, so most stepped into line. The parliamentary democratic system's purpose was no longer to incrementally transform capitalism, nor even to regulate and manage its deep economic processes, but simply to curb some of its more destructive outcomes, and ensure the health and wellbeing of the population within the socioeconomic system as it stands. All attendant institutions – media, education, local government and so on – were given the brief of advocating and realising the ideal of a well-managed and ultimately fair capitalist system. Significant change was, apparently, no longer necessary. Capitalism would, in time, give us everything we could reasonably hope for. From this point onwards it became compulsory and simultaneously beneficial for all attendant institutions – especially media and academia – to demonise and caricature the dream of democratic socialism and promote the idea that it would somehow inevitably lead to Stalinism.

One of the outcomes of this epochal shift in the meaning and practice of politics is that the domesticated vestige of old confrontational politics is now restricted to the campaign for 'social justice' – a combination of policies such as anti-discrimination, minimum wage levels, the continuation of welfare payments and various public services and equal opportunities for all to engage in the highly charged battle for wealth and prestige. Social justice is to be funded not by the fundamental reorganisation of rights to ownership, control and economic participation, but by taxation, which is to be maximised by closing some of the loopholes that allow evasion and avoidance. Injustices are still recognised, and something that looks like the raw energy of struggle still crackles throughout the social body. However, this energy finds an outlet only in the fragmented and fully incorporated disputes between various intersectional groups – women/men, old/young, gay/straight, black/white, indigenous/immigrant and so on.

The general idea is that the traditional oppressed losers can oust neoliberalism's winners from their dominant and privileged positions by flattening out existing advantages and disadvantages in capitalism's competitive socioeconomic system. But the collective spirit to be found within and between these cultural groups is possibly even less solid and reliable than that which constantly let down the working class in the old class struggle – a forlorn yearning for real solidarity in a dominant culture that is, after all is said and done, little more than a struggle between landless, anxious and highly competitive individuals.

This milieu of shifting alliances and hostile relations within and between fragile interest groups in today's competitive individualist culture shows us quite clearly that the term 'social justice' is a misnomer, and that the benefits of 'balancing' advantages and disadvantages can be received in usable form only by individuals who are *a priori* willing to compete against all others. The transition from social liberalism to neoliberalism was clearly marked by the practical establishment of the principle that the individual's self-interest and security must be prioritised before any form of altruism could be considered. However, the maintenance of a tolerable degree of civilised social order in the transition to neoliberal capitalism relies on the system's ability to sustain the illusion that a reasonable degree of social justice is always possible in the near future, even though it has never been truly established in any palpable form in the past.

Under this spell most people keep trying with widely varying degrees of success to achieve the goal of individual freedom and prosperity. The American Dream, now the Global Dream, was founded on the fundamental myth that, no matter what our circumstances might be, any or even all of us can make it if we try hard enough. In a nutshell, the capitalist economy is to be driven forward by totalising economic insecurity in such a way that people find self-interested practice almost impossible to refuse. It harnesses the ensuing human energy, constantly generated by the need to escape the trap of permanent anxiety, to regenerate and evolve. Social peace is to be maintained by ensuring that individuals believe they are not disadvantaged, or at least that they will not remain disadvantaged, in their efforts to achieve prosperity, freedom and security. A detached observer could be forgiven for thinking that stoking anxiety in economically insecure individuals while expecting a fragile and unworldly illusion backed up by a clumsy security state to keep them in order is perhaps, on balance, a bit of a high-risk strategy. Nevertheless, neoliberals assumed that the majority would buy into it, and any trouble caused by the minority could be kept in check by an uneasy combination of welfare and repression.

The election of the old-school democratic socialist Jeremy Corbyn as the leader of the Labour Party in 2015 cast into doubt the assumption that the bulk of the population have accepted the system as it stands. Initially, neoliberals of the right and left tried to respond to this democratic decision with calm. However, they were unable to repress their hysterical fear for very long. One of their main concerns is that Corbyn has attracted thousands of new members to a Labour Party that had been almost totally neoliberalised since the Blairite coup in the early 1990s. He has also caused a stir among the nation's young by promising a return to some of the old Labour left's democratic socialist principles, which were built on measured altruism rather than naked self-interest.

This change of heart by a significant number of young people suggests that post-war liberalism's vastly expensive and highly coordinated ideology machine is no longer as effective in the task of reproducing the 'no alternative' doctrine as it once was. It has also become apparent to our post-political social managers, who, for nearly 40 years, have been trying to play down the gravity of localised social problems, that young people are attracted to the Corbyn phenomenon by neither naive idealism nor rational choice, but by a significant change in their real socioeconomic circumstances – a descent into or at least too close to the reality of precariousness compounded by a dark vision of an uncertain future. The deleterious outcomes of the neoliberal experiment have pushed citizens' perceptions significantly closer to their current reality than liberals – especially neoliberals – like it to be.

The precarious position of youth in the neoliberal economy across the world is well documented (Winlow and Hall, 2006, 2009, 2013; Lloyd, 2013; Smith, 2014; Horsley, 2015; Winlow et al, 2015), but it seems that they increasingly understand their lives and their position in the context of global warming and climate change, mass migration, ecological destruction, resource depletion, terrorism, technological development and the prospect of permanent under-employment, poverty and widening inequality, financial instability and crashes, institutional corruption, the withdrawal of welfare and the numbing vacuity of mass-mediated consumer culture. This new reality of general insecurity sets the context of fear, a fear generated not simply by media scaremongering but by the often painful and worrisome experience of everyday life. The refusal of neoliberal media and academia to talk honestly about our precarious future intensifies this fear and creates space for conspiracy theories, the consolidation of pre-existing prejudices and the construction of various scapegoats.

Those occupying the most precarious and humiliating positions will, of course, experience this fear in its most intense form. They sense its connection to reality more clearly than those whose immediate prospects are better. The relentless pressure to change in accordance with the cultural rules that determine positions in the socioeconomic hierarchy operates disproportionately according to wide variations in the ability and willingness to accept liberalism's fundamental meritocratic illusion and rebuild identities according to new adaptive demands.

The result is mutual fear and contempt, initially generated by the shift into a competitive individualist culture, but structured and exaggerated across a new division between those who are either adapting successfully or adapting badly. This binary division, always present but now fundamental, undercuts the whole 'intersectional' matrix of class/gender/sexuality/ ethnicity/age, etc. However, it remains closely related to class. One could argue that the onus should be on the successful liberal middle class to change first by ditching their belief in identity politics and using their still potent cultural influence to revive genuine politics, a politics capable of intervening in the world to alter our present trajectory. However, the liberal middle classes are extremely reluctant to do this. Their competitive advantage would be threatened, and they may lose the moral high ground, which not only enhances their prospects in the social administration system but also allows them to feel good about themselves and face the future.

Thus the onus remains on the shoulders of those least able to transform themselves or bring back real politics. We continue to see the accelerated disintegration of the former working class as individuals break away from the dying body to take their chances in the competitive market. Only lumpen groups stay put and remain faithful to a vague cause that seems to belong to a devalued non-commemorated past that is quickly fading from memory. Among some, all that is left is the suite of conceits and prejudices once systematically encouraged as the foundation of their identity and cultural capital in the era of Empire by the very same dominant class that now enjoins them to jettison it, and the delusional hierarchy built around the fantasy of the obsolete aristocracy of labour. But in the absence of any real prospects at all – their situation still deteriorates as the increasingly automated economy accelerates towards the objective limits of growth with worsening symptoms of permanent under-employment, a diminished safety-net and a competitive culture of unprecedented intensity – this old fantasy is infinitely more comforting than the truth. It is also infinitely more inspiring than the ineffectual politics and relentless cultural condemnation offered by the liberal middle class. So they hang on to it for dear life. And in the current context, who can blame them for doing so?

The monster returns

It looks like neoliberal capitalism has picked a bad time to depoliticise its population and propagate the 'end of history' myth. But the system's managers were perhaps only dimly aware that as they depoliticised the population, they also placed their own legitimacy at great risk. Having denuded themselves of all the institutional power necessary to combat today's worrying and at times unpredictable sequence of extreme phenomena, which augurs the slide into a precarious future for its citizens, the system's managers have left themselves with only one weak response. They must attempt to neutralise the fear generated by experiential reality with an equal and opposite fear generated by presenting scary visions of the totalitarian repression that will inevitably accompany any attempt to transform the socioeconomic system. The system's institutional apparatus, which now works across the full spectrum of truncated residual politics, is geared up to spring into action at the slightest hint of the return of political passions and serious intentions.

The British media's reaction to Corbyn's success was a particularly crude and spectacular condensation of this knee-jerk. Even though he has been affirmed by a relatively small proportion of the voting population, the explosion of derision and demonisation from the liberal left and liberal right sections of the mass media presented us with a clear picture of just how sensitive this reactionary mechanism is, and just how much the values and discourses of British culture and the fulcrum of British politics have shifted to the right in the neoliberal era. We have come to expect the traditional right-wing press to demonise anything remotely associated with full-blown socialism with as much venality and crudity as it can get on to its pages, but more telling was the enthusiasm with which the left-liberal media joined in the demonisation of Corbyn, criticising and smearing him in ways that were only very slightly more subtle. Forty years ago, talking about Corbyn as he championed local council politics, the trade union movement, identity politics, human rights and world peace, the media placed him firmly left of centre but certainly not 'far left', a category usually reserved for communists, Trotskyists and other groups associated with Marxist-Leninist views. Corbyn's way had always been based on peaceful symbolic protest and democratic political argument rather than confrontation, but in article after article published by *The Guardian* and other left-liberal media, he was unsubtly and at times hysterically associated with the usual Cold War demons – Stalin, Pol Pot, Mao, and so on.

The message was clear – the old state-centred communist system was economically dysfunctional. It was also the perpetrator of mass murder and the totalitarian repression of human rights and civil liberties, and therefore it should once and for all be consigned to the dustbin of history. Somehow Corbyn represents the return of this slain monster as an idea in the 'public consciousness', if indeed such a thing exists in today's fragmented post-social milieu. The apocalyptic warning for mass consumption is that because all forms of collective ownership and control will inevitably lead us down the path to catastrophe, can we take the risk that Corbyn might lead us there? Pressing the claim that Corbyn is unelectable with enough regularity and intensity to reveal their deep fear that if things get even a little worse for the insecure working population he just might not be unelectable and end up as prime minister, the left-liberal media brought its double-barrelled scaremongering gun to bear on the issue – to continue with Corbyn as leader would mean something too close to totalitarianism and economic dysfunction if he gets in, and uncaring Tory rule for the foreseeable future if he doesn't. The right-liberal and left-liberal media can be distinguished by their approaches to issues such as welfare, multiculturalism and taxation, but when faced with even the remotest chance of the return of anything like real left politics, they become one voice.

The response from British academia was on the surface more balanced and measured. Pockets of tentative support for Corbyn suggest that academia might be one of the institutions that can act as incubators for a revived politics, but it is currently wilting after nearly 40 years of intense neoliberal pressure to depoliticise its research agendas and public messages. Academia's specialist sociopolitical disciplines of Social Sciences and Humanities have been driven along this path by conforming to external and internal pressure to replace real politics with liberal identity politics and social administrative matters such as health and wellbeing. The stock response to those who advocate the return of real politics is to complain that they define politics too narrowly. This is an intellectual symptom of the illness that, often following the fragmentary hyper-idealist theories of Foucault and the post-structuralists, has redefined and atomised the political into such a broad spectrum of diverse cultural and administrative micro issues that it has ceased to exist as an effective historical force.

It is difficult to understate the pressure that now bears down on the contemporary academic working in these specialist sociopolitical disciplines. The external pressure from neoliberal managers to chase research income from funding bodies restricted to social administration issues sits alongside the internal disciplinary pressure to place all analyses in frameworks constructed from an array of approved liberal–pluralist theories that confuse, misinform and mollify rather than enlighten the students and the public. The only class injustices to which academics offer a full-blooded response are the withdrawal of equal opportunities and welfare, and the constant stigmatisation of the poor by the dominant right-wing faction of the corporate mass media. Put these things right and the working-class multitude will somehow rediscover its confidence and solidarity, and the wheels of resistance and social transformation will grind back into gear. Well, maybe.

As one moves up the governmental, academic and media systems, the class hierarchy becomes clear – almost total liberal middle-class dominance. There is room for some working-class individuals, but only if they conform, and more often than not they are restricted to the lower echelons of the hierarchy. In academia's Social Sciences and Humanities disciplines, the most important for political education, a hierarchy dominated by the ideologies of right-wing and left-wing liberalism is reproduced by league tables, gross inequalities in research income and the maintenance of prestige among a snobbish population keen on introducing their children to the right social networks. The liberal mass media assist by promoting the work of established liberal intellectuals to the status of global stars, despite the predictability and mediocrity of their work. Liberals will fully accept individuals in the higher echelons of the hierarchy only when they become fully like them in the display of cultural and symbolic capital – people from the former working class now know this, and many pre-emptively adopt the symbols of conformity as early as possible.

The sociologist Pierre Bourdieu did not explain his core concepts of habitus and the actor's struggle for forms of 'capital' with sufficient clarity, and he wrenched both out of their shared political context, but he was intuitively right about the way symbols are used to gain entry to class hierarchies. Middle-class liberals offer working-class organic intellectuals a conditional portal to a better life and a little more political influence, but in return the latter's roots and their ability to represent their historical position in the system must be compromised. This is the perennial trade-off. The liberal middle class has been systematically erasing working-class politics and culture from the map by recruiting and transforming their articulate potential representatives. The first thing the working-class Eliza must discard is not her anger – this is allowed as long as it's not too forcefully expressed or aimed too accurately – but her intention to clearly represent and explain the ugly forms of fear, anger and hatred growing in the remnants of the old working class. To do so would launch us on a revealing intellectual investigation of what really happened to post-war politics and culture, and how to change things around at a fundamental level. This is not what the liberal establishment wants.

The systematic demonisation programme promoted across the spectrum of liberal institutions marginalised any discussion of the old left's principles – class struggle, state power, collective ownership, economic planning and guaranteed economic participation. One of Corbyn's early proposals, a national investment bank, championed by economic historians such as Robert Skidelsky and once proposed by Labour politician Bryan Gould and his Full Employment Forum in the early 1990s, has, as far as we can see, been quietly placed on the backburner. This could lay the institutional ground for a fundamental challenge to private banks' entitlement to create and target investment capital. Without serious investment and viable livelihoods communities cannot be revived. Such vital political and economic moves are now secondary to talk about discourses, narratives, intersectional identities, stigmatisation and so on; talk about the real forces, structures and processes that create and reproduce our reality has been replaced by talk about talk. For instance, Busher's (2015) explanation of the EDL is based on the group's internal 'narratives' and 'discourses', with only a brief allusion to political economy and the harsh experience of systematic socioeconomic relegation, cultural derision, betrayal and the absence of true political representation. It is in this context that the working class's identity – its idea of itself as a group, its prospects and its position in the social structure – is formed, not simply in the decontextualised interaction of signs and symbols.

The 'narratives' of groups such as the old industrial working class do not float like children's stories in an imaginary realm disconnected from reality; they pivot on quilting points of concrete universals, slices of a reality that have often been so harsh and insecure that they demand the constant testing of all political narratives and promises against them. The ability to appease and control this group was dependent on real improvements to wages and general living conditions over the decades of the industrial era, and on the ability to bring the capitalist-imperialist myth close enough to reality to cause significant effects at points of convergence where it really mattered. This is the group least susceptible to a detached mythos that jars against their quite easily perceivable reality, and thus they are understandably suspicious of all narratives other than their own. Consumer culture works very effectively as an alternative and economically functional mythos throughout the general population, but it requires some money or criminal wherewithal to participate, so there are some locales where it simply intensifies feelings of insecurity, humiliation and betrayal (see Hall et al, 2008). Where analyses of the context of poverty and marginalisation are conducted by the liberal left they are usually romanticised, placed in an overly optimistic framework of meaningless concepts such as resilience, reflexivity, values, organic politics, subversion, the leaderless multitude and the moral economy – all fanciful inventions of an older generation of left-liberal academics, and faithfully reproduced by a younger generation of this privileged occupational class.

Cultural and institutional power

Middle-class liberal domination of working-class thought and politics is not new. In 18th-century England, riots were usually symbolic protests about single issues such as food prices and religious rights. There was no real thread to connect these issues, and no articulate political discourse that could represent the working class's collective experiences, their position in the socioeconomic system, their potential as a historical force, or their struggle against the ruling class. From the 1880s, when the Marxist-inspired Social Democratic Federation organised riots with clear political symbolism, to the 1970s, when militant factions wielded some influence in the Labour Party and the trade unions, the English working class had at least some contact with political concepts they could use to understand the capitalist system and their place within it. The clearest and most powerful concepts came from the Marxist stable, but throughout the late 19th century, and the 'short 20th century', when the threat of communism loomed over the world, the English working class showed little enthusiasm for full-blooded conflict and revolution.

The sources of this reticence were internal and external. The leading working-class voices in the Independent Labour Party, such as John Burns, Havelock Wilson and James Keir Hardie, had links to the Christian Temperance movement and were hostile to communism and full-blown socialism. Both movements were eventually overshadowed by the Labour Party, which also rejected Marxism and drew its intellectual sustenance from the firmly middle-class Fabian Society. Just as liberal 'progressives' did in the USA as they reacted with fear and loathing to the growing electoral threat of Eugene Debs' Socialist Party of America in the early 20th century, the Fabians worked hard to become the dominant intellectual influence on the English working class, infiltrating their fledgling Labour movement and, with fine words that conjured up visions of a fairer capitalist society in the near future, gently inveigling them away from Marxism and back towards the moralistic reformist discourse favoured by the liberal left. Any working-class organic intellectualism that might have developed into a full-blown mythos with the English working class at the centre, and which might have inspired the construction of a conceptual schema that could explain their position in the world from their own historical and structural perspective, was suffocated and displaced in the early stages of the Labour movement.

The liberal middle class immediately levered itself *in loco parentis* to the fledgling working-class labour movement. In an attempt to mould the politically aware among the working class into their own idealised image, they became their tutors and assessors, not their political representatives or advisers, in their attempt to construct a framework of intellectual concepts and political strategies derived directly from their own structural position and everyday experiences. The English working class had always had to struggle against a dominant liberal-conservative political discourse that was relentless in its propagation of the social and economic value of the bourgeois entrepreneur and the relative merits of the capitalist system. However, this struggle became virtually impossible as their own embryonic intellectual culture was appropriated by a left-liberal discourse that simply could not speak their experiences, locate their coordinates in the system, capture their interest or stir their blood. Under this suffocating patronage they could not develop a narrative with any mythopoetic power, while their role in the dominant narrative was deemed heroic only when associated with the grateful and enthusiastic adoption of middle-class values and cultural tastes. Their position was that of the perpetual pupil, the Eliza Doolittle to be educated and refined by Henry Higgins before she was allowed to think and act in the world under her own steam.

True working-class organic intellectuals could rarely hold anything more than marginal positions in middle-class institutions – an exception such as Raymond Williams was acceptable because he reconstructed himself as a cultural romantic and humanist to displace and temper the more confrontational elements of his Marxism. When unreconstructed working-class politicians achieved positions of power they insisted that things should get done, so, after the era of Aneurin Bevan – an effective working-class politician, but still restricted to the position of tokenistic understudy – the effort to weed them out of positions of power was redoubled. Eric Heffer was one of the last honest and confrontational working-class heavyweights in the Labour Party, while the more suggestible John Prescott, Deputy Prime Minister during the Blairite era but never really considered as material for prime minister, represents the permanent institutional tokenism that has now become the norm. During the course of the 20th century the English working-class left was carefully disrupted, occupied, diverted and incorporated to become what Orwell called a 'controlled opposition'.

This is not to say that middle-class left-liberal narratives are entirely wrong, conspiratorial, wholly oppressive or orientated entirely to the reproduction of dominance. They speak quite genuinely of fairness, they occupy a sub-dominant position in the overall structure, and in many quarters, such as the mass media, struggle to be heard at all. But it *is* to say quite clearly that because left-liberalism pretended to be the working class's true patron and representative in opposition to the capitalist power bloc the betrayal appears to be worse. Their narratives do not capture with any representative clarity the long experience of the traditional working class or their recent traumatic expulsion from the industrial capitalist system's productive base.

The liberal left colonised the sub-dominant position in the sense that they have successfully occupied the space in which organic intellectualism and political representation could have flourished. The middle-class liberals' struggle for discursive dominance was a negative and perhaps even reluctant struggle; they sought dominance not for its own sake, or even for its immediate rewards, which in some cases were relatively paltry. The objective was to prevent the growth from raw, unmediated roots of an elaborate and sophisticated working-class political narrative that could have been vengeful and dangerous, that might have found its own intellectual feet and led to direct class confrontation or the damaging occupational refusal that would have seized up the gears of a capitalist economy on which the middle class have always depended for their economic security and social status.

All left-liberal institutions have habitually failed to listen to public discourse, often portraying it as a moribund 'common sense' to be transcended by their own inevitably 'brilliant' freewheeling analyses. Clear representations of working-class experiential realities have been marginalised. Only representations carefully filtered through left-liberalism's sanitisation process are allowed through for dissemination by the sub-dominant institutional matrix. Theoretical frameworks are carefully attenuated, but compulsory empiricism is the principal blocking mechanism used to keep out the stark realities that might destroy the liberal left's romantic images of cultural rebellion and stir some real political action.

Slavoj Žižek's well-known critique of Noam Chomsky provides us with a classic example. In the late 1970s Chomsky assumed that the Khmer Rouge was a force for liberation in Cambodia because the data available at the time could not prove that it was, in fact, a regressive ultra-conservative force masquerading as communists and involved in mass murder. The stock left-liberal assumption must be romantic until proven otherwise, so Chomsky chose to portray the Khmer Rouge as what he wanted them to be. However, all Chomsky had to do to get the gist of the real situation, suggested Žižek, was to put his ear to the ground, listen to the public discourse that had grown around the concrete experiences of Khmer Rouge atrocities, and use it as a guide for further investigation. Similarly, the English liberal left assume that even after decades of their own systematic domestication of working-class intellectualism and politics, an autonomous, resilient and proto-political working class still exists because the empirical data they have to hand suggests very little to the contrary. However, it has to be said that Chomsky later admitted his mistake. The liberal left's mistake is more long running because they refuse to admit it, and continuously produce the type of data that from its initial conceptualisation is tailored to affirm their ontological, ethical and political assumptions.

The crime-ridden communal degeneration and abject condition of specific pockets of former working-class residential areas in the UK is denied because supporting data is never generated and the liberal left don't listen to the everyday public discourse of the very people they are supposed to represent. Thus explosions of criminal activity and spikes in crime rates occur from what seems like nowhere, out of the darkness created by systematic empirical manipulation and epistemological denial. The most epistemologically destructive of all the left-liberal discursive devices – the 'moral panic' theory – constantly diverts the inquiring gaze and prevents the people trapped in abject circumstances from true representation. Although blame is constantly laid at the door of the mass media, it is the liberal left itself that secretly regards uninitiated members of the public as a mob of ignorant alarmists, the willing consumers of right-wing media sensationalism.

Those who gain access to impoverished neighbourhoods must always present a positive image of the poor – their altruism, sociability, resilience and sense of social justice. Hatred, inarticulate rage and examples of social breakdown and sheer desperation must always be presented as aberrations. Regardless of its rigour or quality, this type of appreciative representation is selected by the left-liberal media and academic research industries to receive the promotion required to compete with the right-wing demonisation apparatus for entry into the public consciousness. The Social Sciences, Arts and Humanities should be specialists in representations of advanced capitalism's realities (see Dave, 2006), but they are so dependent on funding by neoliberal governments and old philanthropic charities, and equally reliant on promotion by the mass media, that their independence has been almost lost and their incorporation into the media spectacle is almost complete. Thus a simulation of political struggle can be staged that legitimises the dominant neoliberal and sub-dominant left-liberal groups in the eyes of their supporters, and gives the more gullible among the public the impression that some sort of vigorous argument over different political solutions is being had.

The only rule that governs this simulated struggle is that under no circumstances should either side portray the plight of some sections of the working class as unrecoverable within the current order of political economy, or the inevitable product of the political choice they both made to comply with the economic logic of the neoliberal capitalist conjuncture. Avoiding clear representations of the inevitably deleterious outcomes of permanent localised recessions, permanent ejection from tenured work and the permanent removal of social status, both sides collude in the creation of an epistemological vacuum, into which the right-wing media flow to promote their ideological messages of voluntarist degeneracy, and the liberal-left media flow to promote the occasional small successes it manages to achieve in its generally unsuccessful philanthropic rescue missions. The absence of clear contextualised knowledge becomes causative, constantly reproducing neoliberal and left-liberal ideologies, preventing clarity in the public consciousness, and constantly stressing that only limited political action in the economy is possible. Pragmatism rules. Any form of socialism or other form of democratic economic organisation would threaten the ruling class's accumulated property and power, and give the global financial apparatus the excuse to further retract capital investment, therefore nothing like this can be done. If what needs to be done cannot be done, there is little point in making the public clearly aware of the true plight of the ejected sections of the working class.

Suffocation of real working-class experience

Between them, the dominant neoliberal right and the sub-dominant liberal left have won a convincing victory. The intellectual life of the working class, a project springing from the unfiltered communication of the experiences of ordinary men and women, and the connection of these experiences to the structural context they inhabit, has been systematically suffocated. The middle class prevented it from flourishing, preferring to initiate the working class into their own narratives, which are remote, arcane, ironic, contradictory and confusing. The representation of working-class experience was co-opted, and reality reworked in their symbolic realm as the product of their own moral and political agency. They were told they had power and influence to change their circumstances when they had none at all – this was the great destructive lie for which the liberal middle class must one day be held to account.

The working class's autonomous intellectual life was shot to pieces on the runway before it could take off. They were persuaded by the sheer ubiquity of liberal representative culture to see their plight, its contexts and its causes exactly how the liberal middle class wanted them to see it – sanitised to divert any thought of direct refusal, confrontational action or wholesale systemic transformation. All of this culminated in the belief that there is nothing positive beyond the borders of capitalism, and that what currently exists will exist forever. Both the neoliberal right and liberal left proclaimed the end of history and the redundancy of the old working-class oppositional discourse. Educated individuals from the working class who offered their services in the construction and dissemination of either liberal narrative were levered up towards – but rarely into – the higher echelons of the system, and had their work promoted as seminal, brilliant, inspiring, heart-warming, and so on. The systematic suffocation of a grounded conceptual schema that could locate the working class's position in the capitalist system and an accompanying narrative that could inspire them to political action, and its replacement by a left-liberal narrative that became increasingly risible and revealing of its own underlying hostility, negligence and fear of confrontation, was the principal reason why the representational culture of the ejected white working class degenerated into cynicism, hatred and anthropomorphic conspiracies.

The process of displacement and incorporation that, as we have seen, had begun in the late 19th and early 20th centuries, was further developed in the 1960s after a small group of middle-class intellectuals had expressed affinities with Soviet communism. As we have outlined in detail elsewhere (Winlow et al, 2015), the CIA became active in a heavily-funded anti-communist project in Europe, not by bolstering the right, but by redoubling its efforts to encourage and promote the non-communist left (see Wilford, 2003). Central to this was the abandonment of class and the turn to language, cultural identity and social movements. By this time the old English working class had very little of their own identity to fall back on. Their own cultural symbolism and evolving forms were rendered 'uncool' (Frank, 1998). Direct class antagonism was judged unrefined and ill-equipped to deal with what appeared to be a rapidly changing social and cultural order. Instead, symbolic subversion and ironic deconstruction became the order of the day. New fronts were opened up in the fight for equality. Gradually, identity politics came to the fore and class universalism receded into the background. The encouragement of the separatist tendency in identity politics was a more subtle variant of the racial segregation that was orchestrated in late 19th and early 20th-century USA to prevent working-class political unification (Stein, 2016). The sanitised post-structural versions of the black civil rights, gay and feminist movements were given the limelight.

Extending Stein's (2016) thesis, it is telling that the crucial issue of political economy was rapidly ejected from each group. Martin Luther King, for example, was very probably shot because of his constant attempt to point black Americans towards trade unionism and socialism, not because black self-identification and social mobility presented any sort of threat to the capitalist system. Early gay and feminist socialist groups petered out of existence as competitive individuals were encouraged by both the liberal right and liberal left establishment to prioritise social mobility and their gendered identities over their class politics. In the face of obdurate homophobic and sexist elements within the old working class, many women and gays welcomed this cleavage. Potentially powerful working-class sections of these identity groups were subjected to precisely the same process of political evisceration and domestication that had been used to depoliticise the old working class, but this was a far easier task simply because class and potential class politics did not reside in the core of their identities.

The Escher-like impossible object of 'identity politics' was promoted and projected across the liberal landscape as the new road to freedom. This new intersectional struggle for inclusion within the existing capitalist system across the matrix of class, ethnicity, gender and sexuality redefined class as just another cultural relation. Like a cross-cut shredder, the intersectional struggle ripped apart potential class solidarity along cultural fault lines as it simultaneously ripped apart potential cultural affinity along class fault lines, ensuring that the political aspect of 'identity politics' would in reality remain impossible.

This overall shift was affirmed and heavily promoted by western mass media and governments. The far left was ideologically conflated with both Stalinism and the far right (for a discussion, see, for example, Popper, 2011; Jacoby, 2013), which had a huge impact on popular perceptions of a structurally orientated left as a potential 'totalitarian oppressor'. The overall outcome of this concerted cultural activity was the decentring and eventual redundancy of all autonomous artistic and intellectual expressions of the working-class perspective. By this stage in the proceedings, identifying with the traditional English working class, which was to suffer its final humiliating political defeat in the Miners' Strike of 1984/85, was becoming hazardous to the individual's ability to maintain even a reasonably stable and prosperous life and a sense of credibility and social worth. In liberal academia the corresponding shift from structural accounts of the socioeconomic order and the structural analogy in the construction of meaning to the pluralistic post-structural model decentred class and political economy. Class, which was no longer the focus of the great historical struggle, was rethought as a loose assemblage of cultural forms rather than a unified political force in history. The biologically grounded unconscious that linked repressed symbolism with innate fear and aggression was also ousted in favour of the flexible and suggestible post-structural unconscious, a model of idealist social transformation that relied on a systematic misreading of Lacan. Marx and Freud were out, Weber was back in, and Foucault was promoted to the heights of global fame as the leading light of a movement dedicated to placing the discursive realm of subjectivity, meaning and cultural mediation firmly in the foreground to overshadow the far less tractable dimensions of political economy, class, ideology and the unconscious.

The mass importation of American liberal thought, with its underlying philosophical concepts and frameworks based on pragmatism and phenomenology, acted as a filter for more sophisticated and politically dangerous European thought. The American liberal-progressivist habit of demonising socialism by placing it in the same breath as fascism was imported into Europe to provide more attractive and subtle support to the conservative right's demonisation programme. Very rapidly it became possible for cool liberal hipsters to demonise socialism without looking like conservative fogeys. The hierarchy of ideas that was constructed as the cultural turn gathered pace through the 1970s, 1980s and 1990s pushed all urgent and realistic forms of working-class representation into the background. The Utopian vision of a defeated bourgeois system replaced by a humble egalitarian future of co-working and sharing was displaced by narcissistic visions of reclaimed identities, unlimited individual freedom and polysexual pleasure and celebrity, while social justice was redefined as the equalisation of opportunities to attain such goals.

The world was remade for conniving, opportunistic individuals as it was unmade for anyone who lacked the confidence, wherewithal, adaptability and entrepreneurial reflexes needed to jump on the chances that fly past very quickly in our accelerated culture (see Redhead, 2004, 2011). The help for those who were constantly outcompeted and left behind was tokenistic, little more than the maintenance of basic welfare and the constant reframing of the working class as the victim of the sort of stigmatisation that justifies discrimination and explains in inappropriately voluntarist terms their failure to leap on board. But this failure is a product of something far more fundamental and systemic, about which the liberal left prefer to remain silent — the permanent economic redundancy of huge swathes of humanity and their subsequent abandonment by both institutional and cultural politics. Where once liberal capitalism subjected the western working class to *discipline*, it now set about arranging its *exfoliation*.

The new cultural politics

The new world of liberal–postmodern cultural politics that grew to dominate the shifting and reconfiguring non–conservative realm from the 1960s onwards firmly advocated personal adaptation as the replacement for any form of social confrontation and wholesale transformation in the realm of political economy. The tradition of institutionalised politics that had at least won the working class some valuable real concessions in the period that immediately followed the Second World War was replaced by the vision of the 'leaderless multitude', which, in stark contrast, has won the working class absolutely nothing. The leaderless multitude is simply a new name for the Hegelian rabble, a loose and uncoordinated body, often hostile across intersectional boundaries, that prides itself on being *against* every single issue they see as problematic, but *for* nothing in particular. The only way for this sort of fragmented quasi-anarchist politics to gain any sort of credibility in broad liberal politics is to be active *against* prejudices such as sexism and homophobia, but far less active in their support *for* big issues such as the democratic takeover of the financial system, permanent employment or the reversal of global warming, which need the institutionalised political authority they seek to subvert and destroy before anything can be done about them.

Movements such as Occupy are visibly against the bankers but not against the system in which the bankers thrive, and certainly present no comprehensible or feasible alternative way to run an increasingly complex, interdependent and unstable global economy. In a new political realm dominated by single-issue politics, the new left has become dominated entirely by the liberal middle class. The residue of the old white industrial working class has virtually disappeared. They are ignored entirely on the field of institutional politics. All they can see in the new system of cultural politics is the very visible support for cultural minorities occurring at the same time as the destruction of the class-based political authority needed to improve their socioeconomic situation.

The current situation of fragmentation and misidentification makes the coalescence of the working-class elements of all the intersectional groups into a powerful political movement very unlikely. The immediate circumstances of the residual white working class are so economically insecure and politically isolated that they will consider voting for any political party that claims, genuinely or otherwise, to represent their interests. Meanwhile, all the liberal power bloc cares about is that confrontational and dangerous class politics do not reappear. Simple divide and rule? Of course. However, now the divisions are not created by presence but by absence – not *positively* engineered in the old-fashioned way by encouraging cultural groups to discriminate against each other, but *negatively* engineered by making the unifying politics that could bring them together look impossible. In this condition, cultural groups will create their own hostile divisions as they are forced to enter into competition with each other. The losers will become more hostile than the winners.

At the core of the cultural dimension of this divisive new world is the Fall from Grace staged by liberal progressivism, the reframing of the white working class from the political agent of historical change, and the saviour of the west from fascism to a regressive anachronism that must be the first to be cast out. If it is possible to imagine such a thing, the fall in the cultural status hierarchy was perceived to be from an even greater height than the real socioeconomic fall that accompanied deindustrialisation, unemployment and insecure employment in the service economy. This abject new identity of history's all-time loser contrasted starkly with their very recent identification with history's all-time winner. It led to such an unbearable degree of humiliation, self-doubt, fragmentation and atomisation that the descent into powerless abjection could not be resisted by the majority. It was simply accepted by many, who were encouraged to do so by the new idealised identities of androgynous, pliable and unpredictable 'pretty things' promoted by the corporate mass media from the 1960s onwards.

The upshot was that in a couple of brief decades a whole history of working-class political language and other forms of cultural expression that represented both the realities of their existence and the seeds of political opposition and social transformation were attacked and destroyed by the shock-and-awe power of the electronically mass-mediated liberal spectacle. What is quite remarkable is the sheer rapidity at which the working class's swagger and confidence ebbed away, and a formerly vital oppositional culture – which had always been chipped away by liberalism, and placed under pressure and marginalised within the working class by conservative forces, yet still survived as a potent force – degenerated into a residue of inarticulate rage and prejudice inhabited by those who failed to grasp the opportunities for adaptive incorporation into neoliberalism's brave new world.

This new residual group of poorly adaptive working-class individuals, predominantly but by no means exclusively white and living in deindustrialised zones, was, from the 1980s, no longer regarded by middle-class career politicians as a viable constituency. In fact, they were regarded as an embarrassment, a sentiment revealed in 2014 by Labour MP Emily Thornberry as she publically humiliated a white working-class male who wantonly parked a white van outside his house and displayed English flags in his windows during the 2014 World Cup. This abject and immobile position contrasts with the flurry of middle-class liberal piety and self-exoneration as they recuperated all the opportunities for economic, cultural and political power throughout all institutions and popular culture that were still available in the wreckage of the old imperial-industrial behemoth of Grand Britannia. This rapid mass appropriation even filtered down to popular music, once the bastion of working-class expression, which is now dominated and run by the privately educated middle class.

The advocacy of immigrants and formerly marginal cultural groups performed vital economic and political functions – the moral justification of a layer of cheap labour and enforced entrepreneurialism and the cultural elevation of incomers who would be less politically troublesome because they lacked the experience and hard-bitten political nous of the old industrial proletariat. The incorporation of incoming groups into a strong oppositional Labour movement, initially the quite successful tactic of the militant wings of working-class politics, could have strengthened solidarity and enhanced the working class's political clout. But opportunistic entrepreneurial elements within the incomers, residual racist prejudices among the working class, and the divisive effect of neoliberal identity politics all combined to make this a very slow and ineffective process with only partially satisfying results.

Of the new intersectional groups pressing their claims as victims and demanding equal opportunities, feminism and the gay lobby, repelled by the sexism and racism that hung on in some pockets of the old working class, were probably the most easily incorporated. While only some of the immigrant groups benefited from an operative degree of historical integration and representation in the upper echelons of the British class structure, the feminist and gay lobbies were awash with it. Thus the division in the latter two groups along class fault lines was very rapid and destructive. Not only did the successful beneficiaries of liberal-progressivist identity politics quickly lose the ability – and we might even suspect the inclination – to represent their working-class victims-in-arms, but the process of cultural splitting helped to destroy the partial solidarity and symbolic efficiency that had once enabled institutionalised working-class politics to perform this function. The success of working-class members of these identity groups was entirely down to them, a product of their own choice and application as wage workers or budding entrepreneurs in the new service economy.

The arrival of liberal-progressive identity politics as the dominant force on the left has virtually destroyed the real politics that could construct a context suitable for enduring solidarity and harmony between cultural groups. The more the liberal left identified with the officially approved victims, the more the old working class saw the liberal left as their principal enemy. In an important sense, the vocal liberal left became the neoliberal right's stooge, taking the blame for any preferential treatment and social elevation from which the victims could be seen to be benefiting. In the ideological dimension this was a classic synecdoche, as successful members of victim groups were placed in the limelight by the media to represent the small part that always in some way misrepresents a far more varied whole, which in this case includes a substantial number of individuals whose socioeconomic position is probably more impoverished and marginalised than that of the white working class.

This was a time of profound social misrecognition. Working-class members of all cultural groups disappeared from each other's view and circle of respect, and found any form of solidarity very difficult to achieve, even in the few places where it was actively sought. In the meantime, the successful individuals from all class positions and cultural groups, as our research has shown (see Winlow and Hall, 2006, 2013; Hall et al, 2008), simply did not care about the social and political consequences of this fragmentation, and disassociated themselves from the broad spectrum of losers.

From a transcendental materialist perspective (see Johnston, 2008; Hall, 2012; Winlow and Hall, 2013; Ellis, 2015), the dominance of the liberal class in the communicative-ideological realm and their serial betrayal of the white working class in the dimension of political economy fed into the destructive process of *deaptation*, a process in which a once-functional ideology and set of practices becomes dysfunctional in a new context. As the white working class's economic function slipped into a condition of historical redundancy, their systematically neutralised combination of political, ideological and cultural resources could neither put up resistance to profound socioeconomic change nor adapt to the new world of domesticated, digitalised consumer capitalism and identity politics. The fundamental problem was the colonisation, disorientation and deradicalisation of these resources by the liberal class. Our interviewees, who had been offered an alien political discourse that simply did not belong to them or speak of them, showed a total distrust of the whole 'communicative class', the 'symbol specialists' who some time ago Jeremy Rifkin (1995) identified as the new ruling class in waiting, and whose dominant social position existed in direct confrontation with increasingly precarious workers. If indeed lies, disinformation, cynical pragmatism, excuses and broken promises are the inevitable products of the political today, in the eyes of the white working class the guileless liberal left became the main purveyor as the neoliberal right worked in their shadow to do the real damage.

Of course, we know that the racial hatred displayed by many of our interviewees is in the idealist sense rooted in the ideology of the British Empire, the ruling class's encouragement of all British citizens to regard themselves as part of the naturally superior race and culture in the world, and therefore deserving of any privilege they may have. But in the material and visceral sense, it is generated by the fear that that these so-called 'inferior' groups are now out-competing and ousting them from the increasingly precarious position they occupy in the economy and social structure. These well-known formulations can certainly serve as the basis of our understanding of racism. But the hatred we found among our interviewees is cranked up beyond even that standard level. The reason for this intense hatred is that the fear and humiliation they already feel has been compounded by the severance of the relationship they once had with the left-identified liberal class that once pushed itself uninvited into their lives *in loco parentis*. The liberal left promised to be their guiding light, like responsible parents educating them and leading them away from powerlessness, rage and violent confrontation into peaceful and effective negotiations that would eventually ensure their prosperity, security and status. Many among the working class were sceptical of both the intentions and promises of their self-appointed advocates, but, because the English working class were more suspicious of hard-line communists and socialists, this relationship endured throughout the 20th century. For a short period in the era of post-war reconstruction the negotiations bore some fruit for the majority. But from the 1970s, as recession bit and the emergent neoliberal ruling class committed to its unforgiving economic logic would no longer listen, the liberal left abandoned its faith in even this pacified version of the class struggle, and repositioned the once favoured working class as just another competitor in the intersectional milieu of cultural groups competing for a finger-hold in the new neoliberal economy.

Christopher Bollas (1997) showed us how the fundamental trigger for enduring feelings of hatred and revenge is the breakdown of trust between the parents, as those responsible for care, and the children, as those in receipt of the care without which they would not survive. The paternal liberal left abandoned the child it had forcefully adopted just as that child's real circumstances descended into chaos and uncertainty. At this point the child discovered that the pacified negotiating stance it had learned from its parents could not prevent the new neoliberal power bloc from throwing it into that chaotic situation, and to compound matters further still to an unprecedented level of desolation, the fickle parent, now suspected of never caring from the very beginning, found new children to take under its capricious wing. The degree of rage and hatred elicited by this overt betrayal is difficult to imagine.

FOUR

Redundant

Enraged by what they perceived as the disappearance of their fickle parent, our contacts had wandered in from various points in the political wilderness to the only loose organisation that promised to represent their interests. Some made their way to the EDL from the field of organised football violence (see Garland and Treadwell, 2010; Treadwell and Garland, 2011). Very few had been active in other right-wing campaign groups (see Copsey, 2010; Busher, 2015). For the vast majority, this was their first foray on to the field of politics. Before getting involved with the EDL, or vocally supporting its politics from a distance, these men had been totally disengaged from our electoral system. They were disinterested in local politics, and generally unconcerned about the broader geopolitical issues of the day. They were bored to tears by the dour uniformity of our liberal democratic system, and had been for many years. They found absolutely nothing of value in it. All they had experienced on its watch was a descent into the insecure margins and the subsequent deterioration of their collective life.

Despite their prolonged dissatisfaction with the political field, they could not summon up the interest or energy needed to oppose it. They cynically dismissed politics as a sham, a racket, a stitch-up. The political culture they saw enacted on their TV news broadcasts appeared a world away from their reality. Those who occupied the incestuous Westminster bubble seemed quite alien to them. Many of those we spoke to were aware of the ability of the Westminster political elite to shape and reshape their environment, job opportunities and lifestyles, but nothing ever seemed to happen. Nothing good at any rate. In their view, things were becoming incrementally tougher for people like them. No matter which party was in power, they felt unrepresented, forgotten and ignored. Soft metropolitan liberals had taken control of politics, and they were busy feathering their own nests at the expense of everyone else. They saw in politics no principled debates, no vision of a secure economic future, no drive to improve the prospects of ordinary men and women, and no obvious commitment to addressing the genuine problems and frustrations they faced. Things were getting worse for people like them. They were sure of it. And from their position, other social groups seemed to be faring much better.

For our contacts, politicians were the architects of these changes. They had decided to let the white working class die. The traditional entitlements of the white working class were already being withdrawn or transferred to other social groups that appeared more in keeping with Britain's new preferred image of itself as liberal, cosmopolitan, forward-looking and pervasively middle class.

Before our contacts became involved with the EDL, they tended not to vote and were unaligned with any of the main political parties. However, the rapid rise of UKIP from 2012 onwards significantly altered this picture. As our research progressed, and as UKIP forced its way on to the political stage in the build-up to the 2015 general election, it became clear that almost all of our contacts who voted did so for UKIP. The rapid rise of the EDL and UKIP appeared to suggest that things could actually change, and that political engagement might actually hold some interest after all. At last, they thought, men and women willing to disregard political correctness and interrupt the stultifying sameness of English politics were standing up and saying what needed to be said. At last, there were voices keen to draw attention to the fact that unchecked immigration had destabilised England's culture and economy. At last, there was now at least some discussion of the patently obvious problems caused by western Islamism. Muslims were unwilling to assimilate, and to make matters worse, they were forcing change on the host culture. They wanted England to adapt to their requirements.

For many of our contacts, the rise of the EDL and UKIP challenged their cynical resignation. For the first time they began to pay attention to the political field. Perhaps it was possible to oppose and topple the soft liberals at the heart of the system after all. For the first time they were able to step away from the compelling immediacy of their everyday lives and attach themselves to a political project that promised to draw attention to those things that provoked their anger and frustration. For the first time they could demand that the media and the polity paid attention to their concerns. They would issue their demands in a manner they saw fit rather than watch them being diluted, sanitised and diplomatically rephrased by middle-class career politicians. They weren't asking politely to be let in. They were going to do it their way, and fuck the consequences.

Ultimately, the politics of the EDL had encouraged them to put aside the possessive individualism of 21st-century consumer culture to join with others in the pursuit of common goals and the advancement of common interests. The importance of this shift should not be underestimated. For the first time they headed out on to the street to demonstrate, and for the first time they talked volubly and passionately about the political issues of the day. At last the gag and the straitjacket had been thrown off, and a long dormant political being had been awakened.

The EDL had identified the object that caused their anger and threatened their lifestyles. Pissed off at the disintegration of your community? Angered by your inability to get a job? Frustrated at falling wage levels and rising workplace competition? Have the vague sense that your status is declining? The EDL had, figuratively speaking, stepped forward and pointed the finger of blame at Muslims, recently arrived immigrants and the religion of Islam. This process of clear and concrete identification liberated these men from their imprecise sense of perennial frustration. A concrete objective focus for their frustration now existed. An embryonic cause had come into view.

Many of those we spoke to had become involved with the EDL in its early days. They suggested that, as the movement began to develop, they had taken a degree of confidence and satisfaction from the discovery that others felt as they did. It gave them a palpable boost of energy. This discovery of what could be their very own fledgling political community encouraged them to push further to see where the path might lead and just how far along it they could go. Others attached themselves to the movement much later. News reports on EDL demonstrations helped draw attention to the movement. They looked on with interest, and began to think about the issues at stake in a more concerted fashion. In such cases, it often appeared that these individuals had been persuaded by the EDL's discourse. The EDL's identification of radical Islam as the force that was polluting England's culture and destabilising its economy resonated widely in white working-class neighbourhoods across the country. In the absence of any feasible alternative, many disaffected and aggrieved young and middle-aged working-class white men began to dip into the EDL's anti-Muslim discourse.

This uncomplicated and immediately accessible account of ethnic corruption, economic competition and cultural dilution provided these men with a very basic means of understanding their frustrations and combating the cloudy and imprecise sense of loss and incremental decline that seemed to enshroud their lifeworld. They suffered, they were told, because of the arrival in England of millions of Muslims who were unwilling to assimilate into the established host culture, and who, in fact, hated the host culture, and hoped to tear it down and replace it with something else. They suffered because their traditional entitlements were being stripped away by a self-interested and patronising middle-class political elite who found the white working class regressive and distasteful. This elite championed 'diversity' and appeared repelled by many of the indigenous population's customs. In order to advance its drive towards equality and openness, this elite hoped to destroy many of England's traditional Christian values, elevate Islam and Muslim immigrants, and withdraw all the remaining privileges of the white native population. Ultimately, it became easy to broaden the discourse and come to the conclusion that they were suffering because radicalised Islam, aided and abetted by a simpering and guilt-ridden white liberal elite, was waging a relentless war against the west and its principles.

The more our contacts listened to the discourse of the EDL, the more they were persuaded. They found considerable utility in the EDL's identification of Islam as the key disruptive force that was destabilising the country. Some really had seen the arrival of Muslim immigrants into their neighbourhoods. There were more Muslim residents, more Muslim shops and services, and more Muslim kids in the local schools. But other EDL supporters we spoke to hadn't been affected in this way. Certainly, their neighbourhoods had changed. Many modern institutions had disappeared, or changed beyond measure, and their neighbourhoods appeared to be becoming more disorganised and diverse. Proximity to Muslims and 'Muslim extremism' certainly wasn't the key issue for many of our respondents.

Many were willing to admit that their principal contact with Muslims related to their role in the local service economy. In most instances this involved local convenience stores and takeaways. We will come back to this issue later. For the time being, it is enough to note that only some of our contacts were pushed, in a straightforward and linear fashion, towards the EDL by the arrival of Muslims in their neighbourhoods. The roots of the EDL's shared and evolving discourse are much deeper than this.

As we saw in previous chapters, all our respondents had felt the deleterious effects of neoliberalism's tectonic shifts in the economy, society and culture. Of this there is no doubt, but in the absence of a popular political discourse that could illuminate this structural change, anthropomorphic accounts were the only option. Somebody somewhere was doing bad stuff to them – that much was clear. In liberalism's imposed political darkness the new cultural matrix and its representatives took the place of structure and system. Again and again we heard accounts of a creeping prejudice against the white heterosexual working class. In a manner entirely suited to the present era of triumphant liberalism, our contacts often presented themselves as victims of a new systemic cultural injustice. Quite often we listened to outlandish conspiracy theories that inevitably led to the conclusion that the country was being sold out to the globalising forces of radical Islam. The white working class was being shunted to the margins where, those in power hoped, they would quietly die out, creating additional space into which the new urban multiculturalism could move. It was obvious, wasn't it? Where once 'the Jews' were plotting to take over 'the world', it was now 'radical Islam'.

Many of our contacts felt that they were rapidly becoming a minority in their own neighbourhoods. They were discriminated against by employers keen to abide by new legal and institutional requirements that related to diversity and equal opportunities. They were marginalised from mainstream culture to the extent that traditional white heterosexual working-class culture and community life were being erased from history. No one cared about them. We heard this observation – 'no one cares' – over and over again. They felt abandoned and forgotten, and some felt vilified, stigmatised and mocked by mainstream multiculturalist media.

The EDL was their Messiah. Until it appeared on their horizon they had no spokespeople to represent their interests. They struggled to access benefits, while they imagined that recently arrived immigrants were immediately given everything they wanted by an indulgent welfare state. They felt the system was stacked against them, and they felt this way at least partly because they could not access the lifestyles they wanted. The status and sense of value they believed was theirs by right remained frustratingly out of reach. Everywhere they looked, others seemed to be getting a better deal.

Some believed that it would be impossible for Muslims to truly assimilate. The cultural and religious differences between Muslims and the native white English population were simply incommensurate. They were not willing to throw away their birthright and cultural traditions in order to become more acceptable to new arrivals, and it was clear that Muslim immigrants were totally unwilling to adopt the cultures of the homeland. Alien cultures, attitudes and beliefs would, therefore, inevitably destroy the traditional English way of life. No progress could be made because both groups appeared to be totally entrenched in their established positions.

Some of our contacts, after hearing the EDL's account of the threats posed by Islam, said that things became clearer to them. This story, they said, apparently "made sense", and everything "kind of clicked into place". They could now see the damage that immigration was doing. They could now understand why labour markets had changed so much. This kind of ideological transmission occurred for the most part in the social and cultural contexts of white working-class life. It had little to do with the new virtual spaces that were opening up on the internet, and more to do with locality, familiarity and personal connections. They used social media to broadcast their own message, not to learn from others. All media were run by wet liberal multiculturalists and not to be trusted.

We could often see this happening right before our eyes. Discussions in pubs would start one-on-one but quickly extend to all within earshot. They drew in the undecided, and all those interested in the declining prospects of the white working class, and the threats posed by immigration and radical Islamic terror groups. Disconnected 'facts' would be presented, and good old-fashioned persuasive oratory counted for a great deal. Those at the centre of such discussions would often use their knowledge of local economic and cultural issues to affirm the logic of their position. Examples would be given of the perceived economic successes of the local Muslim population. Further examples would be given of welfare-dependent Muslim households in which no one appeared to speak English. The erection of new mosques often caused a huge amount of ill feeling. Fathers would speak of sending their kids to schools in which there were large numbers of recently arrived immigrant children who couldn't speak English. Some claimed that these schools had abandoned traditional Christian festivals and that English children were being forced instead to learn about other religions and cultures.

The empirical veracity of all of this didn't really matter. Over time, this anti-immigrant and anti-Muslim refrain worked its magic, and sceptics were won over. Younger men listened and laughed along with the older men who held sway. The ascendant discourse of the EDL immediately chimed with the worldview of some and, over time, it persuaded many others. But this discourse was not simply a disconnected 'narrative'; it was a managed suite of synecdoches, selected parts of reality presented in a specific way to represent a whole truth that is always more complex and expansive. However, it is not simply a pack of lies, and this is what gives the synecdochal discourse enduring ideological strength.

It is worth reiterating that for years our contacts had carried with them a sense of frustration and anger. Although this anger could be repressed and forced into the unconscious, it never simply evaporated. Now, with the help of the EDL, the discarded white working class had found what they were looking for. Many others like them agreed, and this agreement provided a degree of reassurance and confidence. They liked being among their peers, and they liked the sense of togetherness and common cause that had developed so quickly. They liked that others were willing to speak about these issues in such a forthright way, and they felt sympathetic to these men and keen to present themselves as equally committed. The new white crusaders had identified their cause, and they were finding strength in each other's company.

The liberal mainstream's angry reaction to their vilification of Muslims only encouraged them to dig their heels in. They hated the liberal mainstream as much as the liberal mainstream hated them. If they upset the cosseted liberals of the metropole, this confirmed that they were on the right track. Fuck them and their trendy ideas. Our respondents weren't going to take it anymore. They had been quiet long enough. They weren't going to be dictated to by a bunch of brainless do-gooders who were too stupid to see what immigration was doing to their country, especially the parts of the country in which they lived and the liberal do-gooders did not.

The EDL's identification of Islam as the force that was disrupting English society equipped our respondents with an identifiable foe. They had found something that could represent the ultimate cause of their anger and frustration. This identification of a cause of their frustration, no matter how flawed, appears to have allowed these men and women some respite from the powerful emotions that overshadowed their social experience. It worked. Their frustrations could be represented in a symbolically efficient political form. They could join with others who were similarly frustrated. No longer did they have to stew over their various frustrations alone. At last they could escape the Real, the terrifying shadow world where everything can be experienced but nothing can be understood or named.

In the rest of this book we attempt to shed some light on these processes. However, before we begin a detailed investigation, we must understand that this sense of frustration experienced by supporters of the EDL is important and very real. It must be taken seriously if we are to develop a detailed understanding of the rapid rise of the EDL in many white working-class neighbourhoods in the early years of the 21st century. It is vital that we keep in mind that the EDL developed against this background of broadly felt anger and frustration, this sense of disempowerment, abandonment and growing irrelevance. To take these frustrations seriously is not to excuse the EDL nor to transform them into yet another victimised community to be placed alongside other victimised communities in what has become an incredibly fragmented and competitive social order. Rather, it is a necessary step towards our goal of constructing a reasonably objective account of the EDL and the development of their anti-Muslim discourse.

I'm properly fucked off and I'm just not going to take it anymore…

Let us start with a rather basic truism: anger and frustration are an entirely understandable response to the growing marginality and redundancy of the white working class. These men should be angry. If we were in their position, any of us, we would be angry too. However, our contacts' identification of Islam as the source of their problems cannot be justified. At least not rationally. We have already explained in basic terms the processes that encourage this identification, but the fact remains that the growing number of Muslims in England has very little to do with the genuine problems faced by EDL-supporting members of the white working class. We cannot emphasise enough that these emotional states spring from actual material changes that have transformed our economy and destabilised the working class's cultural and communal life, and not simply from detached post-structural 'narratives' or 'discourses' that create meaning in the play of signifiers. You may feel disgusted by the racism of the EDL and entirely unsympathetic toward its political project, but it makes no sense at all to suggest that the frustrations that have driven so many to adopt the discourse of the EDL are somehow illegitimate, irrelevant or in any way 'unreal'.

The English working class, which has always been made up of many ethnic and religious groups, has, for over 30 years, suffered greatly as a result of neoliberal political and economic reforms. The fathers and grandfathers of many we spoke to had worked in the traditional productive economy in one capacity or another. These jobs were often dangerous, and they were not always particularly well paid, but they were stable, at least in comparison to the forms of working-class service work that predominate today. Crucially, traditional forms of industrial work often possessed a significant degree of positive symbolism. It was possible for some members of the industrial working class to feel that their labour was important and valued. Those who worked in some manual occupations were accorded significant status. Skilled work often provided a sense of accomplishment and a sense that the product of one's labour was genuinely useful and occasionally beautiful. Furthermore, the industrial working class was encouraged to believe that, in its daily labours, it was contributing to the nation's progress. The products of their labour were once exported all over the world. They were the economic backbone of the country. They were vital, and they were wanted.

The toil of individual workers was more than a means of acquiring enough money to eat and pay the rent. It was connected to a broader historical project that moved an entire class away from the poverty of the past toward something better that lay in the future. Industrial workers and their families were able to live relatively satisfying lives, despite their lowly station. They could grow old with a genuine sense of intergenerational progress, safe in the knowledge that their kids would fare a little better. There remained some semblance of organic cultural life, despite the fact that, as the 20th century advanced, this appeared to slip further and further into the distance. Crucially, workers did not always feel compelled to take on the fight for upward social mobility. The community life that developed in many working-class neighbourhoods was, as it stood, a considerable source of value for ordinary workers and their families.

During their childhood our contacts looked on the economic fortunes of their fathers. They recognised the sense of stability and continuity that appeared to characterise the lives of the modern working class during that era. For many, this stability and continuity underpinned a golden age for the traditional working class. Some painted a picture of their parents' lives that seemed quite serene, with established routines, clear roles and supportive relationships interspersed with occasional indulgences, family and neighbourhood gatherings, and the earthy pleasures of common culture. For others, the family home was anything but serene, but that didn't stop these men believing that the lives of their parents and grandparents had been more stable than their own. Besides, they looked on with envy at the serene stability enjoyed by others in their vicinity, which in their eyes only increased its value. Everyone appeared convinced that earlier generations had access to something that was of huge importance but had recently disappeared. Some talked in general terms about a sense of pride and respect. Others talked about orderliness, neighbourliness and a sense of community cohesion. Some of our more articulate contacts briefly and sporadically expressed the belief that it was the collapse of traditional industry that had prompted this loss of substance. But, for generations discouraged from identifying and dealing with the deep political and structural causes of their life experiences, many others immediately began to identify immigration and radical Islamism as the forces behind their downfall.

Our contacts knew that there had once existed stable labour markets and rewarding work, and they were painfully aware that these labour markets were now gone. Some continued to work in the manual trades but tended to feel anxious and resentful about increased labour market competition, falling wages and the ubiquity of short-term contracts. Others were forced to compete for unrewarding and insecure jobs in the service economy, jobs that tended not to pay enough money to raise a family. Yet, remarkably, obeying liberalism's command not to stray on to forbidden territory, they were consistently and sometimes aggressively reluctant to make any attempt to connect this to the tectonic shift in the underlying neoliberal economy. Most of our contacts were committed consumers, and they liked to display the outward trappings of success. Many wore designer labels, even though, quite often, this appeared to be a defensive action geared towards simulating a vestige of the social status they had lost.

We spoke often with our contacts about their local neighbourhoods. We discussed in detail the changes that had occurred in the places they knew best. In every case the story was one of decline. They talked of a stable local culture ripped apart by the arrival of disreputable and foreign interlopers. They talked about welfare-dependent households, crime, anti-social behaviour and endemic drug dealing. They talked about disused buildings, vandalism and the gradual degeneration of their neighbourhoods into wrack and ruin, and the complete absence of any form of authority that might seek to prevent further degeneration or begin the gradual process of improvement.

David is 42 and lives in rented accommodation on the edge of the estate on which he was born (all the data contained in this book has been anonymised; all names have been changed and all locations have been disguised). He proved to be one of our most important guides throughout our research. We spoke to him often, and he introduced us to others who felt as he did. He has this to say:

> 'When I left school I got a job straight away. It was no bother in them days. Straight into Pickering Manufacturing, on the [production] line. It was great. I loved it. I mean, it was proper hard graft and fucking boring as shit but the money was great for a lad at that age. We had a laugh. I liked it. I had mates there and it was just, well, it was good times, that's all... I lasted four years there. [The factory shut down.] I got some other factory work but by then everything was fucked. I went all over working short contracts. It wasn't too bad but nothing steady. Since I hit about 30 [years old] things have been fucking murder. I'm a good grafter but there's fuck all for me to do. You can get a job maybe in a call centre or in a shop but I can't do that. It's the money. I'm not that bothered now what the job is. It's all short term. I need regular

hours. I need to earn. I can't just sit waiting to get an hour here, an hour there… For Christ's sake, I'm not a kid anymore. I need a proper job.'

David works as security guard. For the most part he works contracts that last between one and three months, and relies on private employment agencies to find him work. Here he explains the problems he faces:

'It's the best I can do. There's fuck all else. I can do alright if I get a couple of month's steady work, but then you're fucking desperate to be kept on, or you're desperate to find something else straight away once you're finished. It's just shit work really. The pay is fuck all. I've got two kids for fuck's sake. How the fuck do to you pay for Christmas, birthdays? It's just a fucking con, isn't it? It's just fucking bullshit. It's not just me… I just need a proper start, something steady. It's not like I'm a young kid, phoning in sick all the time, looking for days off and that. I've never been any bother. Always tried to find work. The whole thing is just set up to take the piss out of people like me.'

This kind of story is ubiquitous. Young Mike is 22. Unlike David, he has no memory of the industrial work cultures that once existed in this locale. Nevertheless, he recalls feeling confident, while still at school, that he would move seamlessly into a stable career in manufacturing or one of the manual trades. Young Mike left school with only minimal qualifications and has been struggling ever since. He has quite a diverse work history for one so young. He worked briefly as a builder's labourer, which he enjoyed very much, but mostly he has found work in the low-level service sector. He has made a number of horizontal moves between employers that often pay close to the minimum wage. In some cases, he left employment in search of a more tranquil work culture, less orientated to targets and constant performance management. In others, he left because he believed there would be a better chance of progressing up through the hierarchy elsewhere. However, underneath all this is a desire for reasonably settled working hours and a wage level to fund an adequate lifestyle. In the last year or so he has been reliant on employment agencies to find him work. This work has, he says, been low paid, transitory and totally unsatisfying. He hopes to find his way into a manufacturing job at some point in the future. He believes himself to be more suited to this kind of work. He doesn't like offices, and hates working in retail. His only income at the moment comes from a part-time job delivering pizzas.

> 'I got a job working with our Tom [his uncle, a local builder] for a bit but he didn't have enough [work] coming in to keep me on regular. I get a couple of days here and there but there's fuck all. My dad was always on at me to get a job and I've tried. I've fucking tried. I worked in a sports shop for a bit. I've done some factory work but it's all short term: a week here, a week there.'

Young Mike is back living with his parents after the end of a romantic relationship. Here he reflects on his work history:

> 'Some of the jobs I've had are just total madness. The way they go on, treating you like an idiot. I've just fucked off a few jobs coz I can't stand being pushed around… It's okay at the moment, because I'm back at my mam's. What I'm doing now is all right really. It's better than being stuck behind a desk until 10 o'clock at night answering phones. The money is shit, obviously, but what can you do? I do okay, I suppose. You've got to do something. It's enough to see me all right and you get plenty of time to just fuck about and that… I know I'll have to find something better, but who knows when that'll come, you know? You've just got to say "bollocks" and get on with it, haven't you?'

David talked in considerable detail about the changes his neighbourhood has seen. He has spent much of his life living there, and knows it intimately:

'You know what it's like around here. I'm not pissing anyone off by telling you what's happened. When I was a boy the school was a good school. People had respect. You didn't see all the shit you do now. People worked. I could take you out that door right now and show you three, four drug dealers' houses. It's just the way it is. It's the way things have gone. You've got drugs all over the place and then you've got people thieving to get money [for drugs]. Nowt against them people [the drug dealers], but you never saw that when I was coming up. It's just all fucked. The place is barely recognisable. Like, you always had lads getting pissed when I was young, but it's different now. It's just not the same. It's not like it was, honest. My dad has had bother [trouble] outside of his house. The police are there all the time, but nothing changes. And all the people what's moved in, people from all over the place. What does that say to the people that live around here? I bet they don't have straight-off-the-boat immigrants moving in where you live do they? [...] It used to be you knew your neighbours. When I was a young one, we all knew each other. Families mixed together and that. I talk to my dad and he says the world's gone mad. He just can't make head nor tail of it. He's got Somalis, Polish, all kinds living up there. It's just fucked, all of it.'

David and Paul have been friends for many years. They still meet regularly in the local pub, and quite often their conversation turns to the problems they face and the disintegration of their neighbourhood. Paul is a gas fitter, and, in comparison to many of his peers, his finances are for the time being reasonably secure:

'I was always told, get a trade. I knew I had to get a job and you had to have a proper trade behind you, even in them days. I done okay compared to a lot of others. There was jobs then, and if you were okay you could get in. As long as you did the graft and didn't take the piss you were okay, really... I've been in work pretty regular. I've been full-time on the books, I've been out contracting, I've worked on the [building] sites. The work is there if you want it and you can graft. That's the problem with a lot of people around here. I agree with him [David], things are fucking hard and there's not a lot [of work] about, but I look at a lot of people around here and they're just fucking proper dirt-bags. He'll not say it but they need a proper kick up the arse. Some want to work and some don't. It's the fuckers that just expect everything for free that's the problem. It's them that end up with the kids in bother, dropping out of school. It's them that end up fucking torturing people with loud music and police calling at all hours… It's people what's come on to that estate, yes, but that's not the only thing. A lot of them people are proper fuck-ups. Some of the kids, I wouldn't want to tangle with them. It's not just there's no work.'

Trevor, another friend of David's, intervenes:

'It's not just round here, you see it all over. People have just given up. They sit on their arses all day, fucking stuffing their faces and watching TV…. All this shit about there's no jobs: of course there's fucking jobs! There's plenty of jobs! Get off your arse, mate, do some fucking work, that's what I say.'

Young Mike:

'The jobs that's out there are fucking shit mate, you wouldn't want to do them.'

Trevor:

'I'm not saying they're good jobs. You've got to take what's there, haven't you? That's the way of the world mate. Get in there, graft, and work your way up.'

Paul, talking mostly to Young Mike:

'Look mate, all you need is to get yourself a decent
start [meaning a decent job]. Then you've got to kiss
arse, do your qualifications, work weekends, whatever
comes up, generally just be a good lad and work hard
and people start to look after you. I'm not saying it's
not hard, but that's life mate. It's survival of the fittest.
No one gave us free hand-outs. It's graft mate. That's
what it's all about.'

Tony is 44 and works in a traditional manual job he would prefer
us not to discuss in any detail. He is reasonably well paid, and
he has worked for his present employer for just over 10 years.
He wears designer sportswear and drives a nice car. Despite his
relative affluence, he is keen to identify the problems that his
neighbourhood and community are facing:

Tony: 'It's difficult around here, isn't it? Look around
you. The place has been going downhill for years.
People are just fed up, that's all. People can't get work.
People have moved away. I moved away, obviously.
That's how it goes. Why would you want to stay now?
What's here, really? What's left? Most of the lads I
grew up with left. The others, well [his voice trails
off].... I used to worry leaving my car parked outside
my mam's. It's just all getting a little wild, that's all.'

Interviewer: 'But this was always a bit of a dodgy
place wasn't it? It was never perfect.'

Tony: 'Well, I suppose. Maybe it's just me looking
back. But I think there were rules then. It was
different. I don't know what it was. There was crime
and that, but I think it was less. There was a bit of
violence but it was, well, there was a lid on it. It was
kind of, there was rules, wasn't there? There wasn't

really bullying and the things what you read in the papers. There wasn't the problems you see now.'

Interviewer: 'What problems?'

Tony: 'Well, all sorts, you know? Look at the place. It needs money spending on it, doesn't it? It needs fixing up a bit. There's rubbish all over the place; you never saw that when I was a young one. It's just, it's gone hasn't it, that sense of community. Maybe it's me being, what do you call it, soft about the past, about it was better when I was a boy. I think if I lived here now I'd be even worse. It's pathetic really. No one cares do they? You've got drug addicts, you've got the drugs, you've got what, no jobs? No future for the kids? Growing up here now's not the best start, is it?'

Interviewer: 'What's caused all this then?'

Tony: 'Well, you know better than me. It's the politicians. They don't care what happens up here. No one cares. There used to be jobs, good jobs. That's the difference. When you've got jobs you've got respect. You've got, what, a future, something to care about? I can't put my finger on it. No one gives a fuck about these people is the truth of it, and things are just going to go from bad to worse. Some of them can't even look after themselves.'

Interviewer: 'So it's politicians not defending jobs then?'

Tony: 'Well, that and everything else. The whole lot of it has just disintegrated. The politicians today are just money-grabbing bastards mate, fucking liars and cowards. You'll never convince me any different. They're just lining their own pockets while places like this disappear. You never hear about this stuff on the news do you? I'm glad I got out when I did

because there's no fixing it now, I don't think...
Look at what they've done. All the jobs are over
in China and wherever the fuck it is. They've just
opened the floodgates and millions have come in,
and when that happens your job is fucked because
there's more competition. It changes everything. The
building game now is full of Polish who charge next
to nothing. The quality is rubbish but people don't
care. They just want it cheap.'

Interviewer: 'You sound a bit angry about it all...'

Tony: 'Well, a bit I suppose. It's only you that makes
me dig it all up again isn't it? I can ignore it mainly.
You just look after number one and keep yourself to
yourself. I have a drink on a weekend, watch the kids
play football. For me things aren't too bad, all told.'

Interviewer: 'So what's all this with the EDL then?'

Tony: 'Well, I went on a protest that one time, but
since then I haven't bothered. It's just got, well, it's a bit
too dodgy now isn't it? I knew some lads who were
involved, and they're right what they were saying:
immigration has been an absolute nightmare. It has
mate, I don't care what you say. You've got to look
through that bullshit about not being racist and, well,
you see what's happened, right? It's not just around
here. Drive out to Middleton, go up to Craghead.
Things is getting worse all over. They've come over
here and jobs have gone. Anyone can see that. But
it's everything else as well. Have you heard about
that Sharia law? You've seen the bombings. I read up
on them grooming cases mate and it made me so
sick I couldn't speak. What a fucking world we live
in now, eh? It's only right that people are properly
fucked off about it. Why should they just swallow it,
why should they keep quiet and let it carry on? [...]
They [Muslims] hate people like me and you. They

do. Some of them might be friendly enough at first but behind all that is hate, their hate. They think all other religions are bullshit and they want rid of them. They think we're infidels, like we're second-class citizens. I can't see what's wrong with saying no to all that, saying this is our country, you know, "fuck you" kind of thing. It's them that's causing all this. It's daft not to defend ourselves. The politicians are doing nothing. They don't care about me and you. They don't care about places like this, or young kids who can't get jobs. They'd rather support the immigrants, wouldn't they? We're the ones in the firing line. I'm just done with it all, it's just bollocks. So that's why I went on the march. I just wanted to. I just wanted to say, if people are standing up against this sort of thing, then I'm with you, you know?'

Interviewer: 'Told you you were angry…'

Tony: 'It's just sometimes it comes to the top, mate. I'm not like this all the time. It's just coming here and seeing all this. It's your fault making me dig this stuff up… I'm not really a supporter [of the EDL] anymore. I'm not going on any more protests. I can't do it with work. If my face gets seen or if you get arrested it's you job isn't it? I can't do it, with the kids and everything. And a lot of them, well, there's just no leadership. They don't seem to know what they're doing. Some of the local lads mean well but you just can't see it going anywhere now. They need to join up with UKIP or something, I don't know.'

David, who we met earlier, offers a narrative of decline very similar to Tony's. Like Tony, he connects perennial economic instability not to neoliberalism's deindustrialisation and relocation programme, but to the arrival of immigrants, and, like Tony, he is keen to draw our attention to the incremental decline of community life in the region's traditional working-class neighbourhoods:

David: 'It's immigration. We're just a small island, for fuck's sake. I've got nothing against a lot of them. A lot of them are just trying to get a better life, but it just makes it that much harder to get work. There's more people. It's obvious. Some of them are working for less than minimum wage, I know they are, cash in hand. It's just mental. Why do we have to keep quiet about it? We're supposed to go along with it but it's not them fuckers who can't get a job.'

Interviewer: 'Who?'

David: 'The rich cunts in the city. On the TV and talking in the newspapers, calling us racists. It's not their jobs on the line, is it? It's not fucking loads of people moving in next to them, is it? They [the immigrants] can't even speak the language. They've got nothing in common with the people. Why the fuck should we just fucking sit back and take it?'

Damien is 22. He was raised by a single mother on a notorious sink estate. He left school with few qualifications and drifted into petty crime. His last brush with the criminal justice system encouraged him to try again at living a legitimate, law-abiding life. He currently works intermittently in a warehouse for a leading supermarket chain. His wages are very low and barely cover the cost of food and heating:

'There's nothing left for the likes of me. What chance have I got of a decent start? There's nothing here. Even if you do go to college or whatever and get qualifications, it doesn't mean you're okay. Half the lads I work with in the warehouse have got the same contract as me, part-time, even with qualifications. I rely on a few extra hours, but they won't give me a full-time contract, just overtime, so they have you over a fucking barrel.

'That's the thing, mate, see where I live it's all fucking Pakis with the businesses, the money. They own the takeaways, and where I am it's all takeaway shops, it's all cash businesses, so they aren't fucking paying in [paying tax] and they're all fucking fiddling the social too. You see them all cruise up in their fucking top-of-the-range Audis and Mercs, all in fucking Armani and Boss gear, I see that every day and I have fuck all. What am I supposed to do? How can I get what they have on minimum wage part time?'

All the men quoted in this chapter support the EDL to varying degrees. However, they all maintain that they are not racist in any generic sense of the term. Their antagonism is reserved for Muslims, and for those they believe have helped to advance the interests of Muslims at the expense of the white majority. David sums up their views:

'Look, the EDL is not a racist organisation. People say this over and over. We're just saying that the Muslims are causing problems and something needs to be done about it. We're not against blacks or anything else. We're not against any other race. We're just saying, look, they're taking over, they're not blending in. They don't want to blend in, don't even want to learn the language. They don't want to change and become like us. They just want to take over this country and, basically, do whatever they want. They want Sharia law, they want to keep preaching about whatever they want, they want their languages taught in schools. And everything else just gets forgotten. The history, all of that. Look, they're not blending in at all, are they? Go on, admit it. Where are they blending in? Instead, we're the ones who've got to change, right? Fuck that mate, fuck that.'

Trevor:

'It's not racist to say that there's too many people come over here is it? What's racist about that? Fair enough, I don't want them moving in next to me, but then they don't want me moving in next to them, do they? Fair enough. Each to his own. I'm not bothered by blacks, Muslims, none of that. Honestly. As long as everyone stays on his own patch there's no bother as far as I'm concerned.'

Paul:

'I'm not racist, not really. Some things I think might come across as racist, but that's just because of the shit state we're in, isn't it? It's just gone mad, all that political correctness bollocks, the fucking thought police telling you what to think and that. I'm just fucking sick of the immigration. That's it, basically. That's the problem. If the government hadn't let every fucker come into the country there'd be no EDL. You wouldn't have miserable fuckers like me in the pub complaining. People wouldn't care about Muslims. I didn't care about Muslims until the bombings started. I didn't care about Muslims until they started putting up mosques everywhere. Now they're all over the place. They're taking over... They say we have to become multicultural, but why, why is that a good thing? It's bollocks to think that people will mix in, and it's bollocks to think that mixing in is always good. Why? I don't get it. What's good about it? What was wrong when it was just white here, and Muslims over there? [...] Politicians talk like they know what's best for everybody, but where's what's best around here? What are they getting right around here? Find one person that'll tell me things are getting better, one person. Everyone knows what's happened. People like us are getting fucked over and no one gives a fuck. Same as always.

'They [Muslim immigrants] come over here and get a council house and they sign on and get all the benefits. And looks what's happening. The system can't cope. We're having to cut back all over the shop. People pay into the system since school and then there's nothing left, no pension, no health, the schools are a mess, everything's a mess. And why? What's wrong with saying the truth about what's happened? You mention immigration and then you've got some fucker stands up and says it's racist to say anything about it? It's bollocks mate, total bollocks.

'People say we're racist but, when you think about it, they're the ones that's racist. They're killing white people just because they're white. They're killing Christians because they're Christian. It's them that's declared a holy war. We are just reacting. If they left it alone there'd be no EDL. Racism's always one-way isn't it? It's always the white man gets called racist. Everyone else does whatever the fuck they want.'

Young Mike agrees:

'I don't give a fuck about none of that shit. It's just, why does it have to happen here? It [radical Islamism] is spreading all over the place, and they fucking hate us! Look at them protesting about the war and that. They fucking hate us… It fucks me off because they kick off out there and then we've got to go and sort it out. Then it's our soldiers getting killed just trying to get things sorted out. But when you see them protesting when the soldiers come back, that's just fucking madness that, total madness. And then it's bombings, and Lee Rigby and fucking paedophiles in Rochdale or wherever it was. And no one is saying anything. The politicians turn up and say they're going to fix it, but everyone knows nothing's going to happen. It never does. It's only the EDL saying anything… Look, if there's going to be a war, let's have a war. Let's just go out there and get it done, you know what I mean? And stop them coming over here, because it's just madness that they keep coming after all that's happened.'

Brad agrees:

'I am sick of the lot of them [Muslims]. I'm sick of their demands. It's all take, take, take. They take the piss out of us, bringing hundreds over through arranged marriages and that, looking after each other and fucking us over. It has to stop; this is England, not fucking Afghanistan!'

David joins in:

'What's happened is just nuts. There's just been too many. There's not many of us left, and who gives a fuck about us? Get your fucking university people to get a petition going about that!'

Young Mike intervenes, and says half-jokingly:

'Ten years from now it'll be all Muslim round here. All immigrant. They'll have the Sharia law, black flags everywhere. There'll be nothing left.'

Away from his friends, David is again keen to discuss local matters. He wants to make it clear that, for him, it is the disintegration of his community that has prompted him to support the EDL:

David: 'When I was young all of this was white Protestant. We had a proper community where people looked out for each other. I'm not saying it was perfect, but it was better than this. Then you get the mixing, gradually it happens, and they tell you it's a good thing, and keep quiet or you'll get called a racist. It's gone hasn't it? And why? Because of the politicians, because of people like you, fucking do-gooders, who only care about immigrants and making sure everyone in Pakistan can come over here and get a council house and a job-seeker's cheque. I'm fucking done with it mate. It's all for shit. What's the point? If something doesn't happen soon, things will just go downhill quicker and quicker."

Interviewer: 'So how do we stop it?'

David: 'We need some proper politicians with some balls. We need to get out of Europe and stop the immigration. We need to defend ourselves better and make sure we get out there and bomb the shit out of these terrorist groups. We need money for the army, and we need money for jobs. But look at the politicians we've got: total waste of space. Not worth a light, none of them. Spineless twats.'

So why support the EDL? According to David:

'The EDL is about the working class. It's about local people. I don't want to vote for them cunts down south. It's about sticking up for our people. Everyone else does it, why can't we do it? The rich stick up for the rich. The Muslims stick up for the Muslims. We're working people. We don't want anyone else taking up jobs here. We don't want them coming over here and taking the benefits.... The EDL, basically, is just a bunch of people who are sick of the way things are going.'

Brummy is 31. He has been involved in football hooliganism for many years. Again, he is very keen to assure us that he is not a racist:

'I'm not a racist, but the country is broke. I can't see why I should pay for fucking interpreters for lazy Muslims who can't be bothered to learn English but are happy to take our benefits. I can't see why, when I've paid taxes all my life, some newly arrived Muslim should get the same treatment as me on the NHS. I can't see why we should pay benefits for "Abu al fucking Hatespeaker", whatever his name is, so he can raise his 10 kids and slag off my country. That isn't racist, that's realist. And why is no fucking politician saying that? I will tell you why; it's coz they couldn't give a fuck so long as they're alright… They [Muslims] can't live like us coz they are not evolved for it. They're simple, made for backward villages in the mountains where they can sit around eating stinking curries and raping chickens. They come over here and ruin England. I mean, would you want to live next to them? I don't. But they're taking over. That's why I want them gone.

'I left school with no qualifications and that. Fifteen, nothing right? Now I see all these Muslim kids, all these Pakis, and they think they can rub my face in things, they can treat me like a cunt, look down on me. They all wear Armani, they all have nice cars, they all have money, but they don't want England to be English anymore, because they want to be in power. They want to take over the world. They fucking do. They have come in and sneakily and they're trying to take over. You look at who is buying the big houses: it's Muslims. You look at who owns the businesses: it's Muslims. The blacks hate them too, because when they get into an area, they take it over. They are buying churches and building mosques on them. What hope is there for white English lads like me now? None. The Muslims are taking it all away.'

Many of those we talked to were particularly disgusted by the Labour Party. For them, the Labour Party was the party of multiculturalism and mass immigration, a party of vapid political correctness and bleeding heart do-goodery. However, in the vast majority of cases, our contacts knew very little about its history.

Certainly, they did not see it as the political representative of the labouring class. Instead, they imagine the party today to be wrapped in the intoxicating, perfumed air of trendy metropolitan liberalism, and staffed by right-on, university-educated, weak-chinned geeky pacifists who know nothing of the pressures of the real world. However, this broadly felt hatred of the Labour Party has not forced Paul into the arms of the Conservative party:

Paul: 'The Tories are just smug Lord Snooty types. Why would they care about what happens up here? They slag the lefties off for letting in the immigrants, but they'll be no better. They know which side their bread's buttered. They're not going to do anything to rock the boat. It's only UKIP that's really saying they'll put an end to it. I'm going to vote UKIP because that's what they stand for. They want to defend English jobs, cut down on fucking immigrants scamming the system and make people think England's not an easy touch.'

Interviewer: 'So why follow the EDL?'

Paul: 'UKIP is different. They're going to do things one way and the EDL do it another. The EDL is really for people like us who are just fucked off with it all. We're going to stand up for ourselves, you know what I mean? We're not debating or talking, none of that, we're saying "fuck you!", you know what I'm saying? [...] I haven't been to many demos but the lads that go, most of them anyway, they're willing to have a bit of a go [he means, they're willing to have a fight], aren't they? That's what this country needs, a bit of backbone. We need to start standing up for ourselves. We're sick of being pushed around... People who follow the EDL will say things that UKIP can't say, things they couldn't get away with... UKIP is like a posh version of the EDL isn't it?... I mean, to be honest, I don't trust them. They'll probably fuck it up.

They're probably liars. But you've got to give them a go haven't you? It's either that or not vote, for me. I'm not voting for any of the others. Never… We'll see how it works out, but at least they're [UKIP] saying they'll stop immigration. We're [the EDL] a bit more hard core. Lots of people just think that it's time to stop fucking about and actually do something… See, with politicians, it's all got to be polite and calm and that. It's got to be, you know, respect people you don't agree with, stuff like that. People I know what's got involved [with the EDL], they know what's really going on. They know about the grooming and gangs of Pakis hanging around schools waiting for young girls. They know about the drugs and the gangs. They see these bastards [he is referring to radical Muslim clerics] standing up in public and saying that we should have the Sharia law and that all white people are evil. Now, for me, there's no being polite with that. You've got to be hard core. You can't fuck about.'

Diane is 39. She is one of the few female contacts we were able to develop. Again, the issue of grooming and the sexual exploitation of vulnerable white girls structured her hatred of Muslims:

'You know, for me it is more about what their men do. You've heard about the grooming gangs. Well, I knew about them because of our Cheryl, when she was in care. Those dirty fucking Paki, Muslim bastards, they tried it with her. They were always around, fucking sniffing round the school gates. It was known about for years before it was ever in the papers. It was common knowledge where I'm from. Look, at any school you see it: fucking young Paki lads cruising by in their cars, targeting the white girls.'

Richie is 36 and has supported nebulous far-right causes for around 10 years. Like others quoted here, he was keen to talk in detail about the disintegration of traditional white working-class community life. Many of our respondents began their analysis of their own motivations in this way:

> 'I remember growing up, we never had it easy. My old man worked in a factory; mam did a few hours in a shop once we were in school. Everyone knew everyone on the estate. It was poor and it had its problems, don't get me wrong, but not like now. There was a sense of community and hope, but that's gone now. Nobody really works; not decent jobs like in those days. Now it is all shop work, and the only shops local are big chain stores, loan places, fast food shops and bookies. It's bleak. There's no work, even labouring on a building site, it's all CSCS [Construction Skills Certification Scheme] cards and massive competition, and if you get a start you're lucky if it lasts a couple of months. Jobs round here are all short-term contracts with no guarantees. Low wages, no certainty. It's no wonder that people feel angry about it.'

Richard's account of community disintegration and the politics of class is strewn with contradictions. Richard earns a significant proportion of his income from drugs sales, but he believes mass immigration is the primary force destabilising working-class communities across England. He briefly mentions 'the system', but fails to follow it up with any clear understanding of what the system actually is or how it works:

> 'Tell you what, not all of us [in the EDL] are stupid. We know the score. We know we are being fucked over by the system and they don't give a fuck about us. It's dog-eat-dog. There's no other way. I actually see the Muslims and I see how underhandedly they look after each other. It's like the lies about moderate Muslims. I don't see moderates. I see more devious ones that secretly support their own. They might not say it but they do it. They might say they don't support terrorism, but every time there is an attack on the

West anywhere, secretly they celebrate and nobody has the balls to point it out. They are like that because they stick together, because any Muslim, the most important thing to them is other Muslims. They are all one and the same. Where is that in my community? We have none of it, no fucking community. It's like everyone taking advantage and out for themselves, the politicians, the bankers, everyone just blinkered and only bothered by their own shit. That scares me, because while it's like that we're sleepwalking into a world where we could wake up under the fucking black flag of Islam. I can see that, that's why we need to get organised and fight back.'

Young Bren doesn't really care about politics. He has no interest in any of the major parties, and, like many others we spoke to, he has no real understanding of the founding principles of these parties and the influence they have had on the development of the nation. To him the EDL is about sticking up for white people:

'It's just all the Pakis coming into the country, fucking everything up. What have they got to come here for? We don't want to be Muslims. We don't want none of that shit around here. Let them stay where they are. I'm not racist but there's just too many of them. And then you see them protesting against the war, you see them shouting at young lads who have gone off to fight, gone off to do their duty, you're got to be fucking kidding haven't you? This is our country. I don't care what anyone thinks. It's right what they're [the EDL] doing. It's just about saying, no, this is ours, fuck off.

'The EDL, well, to me it's about having a laugh and just telling the Pakis to fuck off. I don't know about any of that other stuff. I couldn't care less. I just don't want them here. I think it's fucking madness that the politicians and everyone else sticks up for them when they're bombing us and taking over all over the place.

I just can't understand it. They're building mosques, they walk around in sheets and people think, what the fuck's going on here? When did that happen? You see them all over. It's fucking nuts, isn't it? You see them, and you're like, whoa! Like you've been transported to Bangladesh or something!'

Paul again:

'Don't forget, it's this Sharia law what bothers a lot of people. What's that got to do with our country? Why can't we just say, "Have it back home, but you can't have it here"? What's wrong with that?

'You have a walk down Thompson Road, have a walk down Lessing Crescent: there's Pakis everywhere. My nan lives down there. Everyone is trying to move out. All the shops have gone, everything's gone. Then you've got your Europeans. Are we living in fucking England or what?'

Conclusion

We sat for hours with EDL supporters discussing these issues. Inevitably, a sense of frustration pervaded our discussions, and we were returned to the same issues again and again. Some of our most cogent respondents talked in considerable detail about neighbourhood decline and the current instability of working-class labour markets. There was often an aching sense of sadness and loss, but these emotions, especially in group discussions, could quickly change into anger and resentment. Our respondents often struggled to accurately identify what had been lost. They talked about the loss of community life and stable labour markets, but they also often seemed to be grasping for something else, something they couldn't quite put their finger on. Ultimately, it seemed to us, they were saddened by the loss of stability as such. To them everything appeared to be falling apart. Throughout their lives they had witnessed what they understood to be a gradual degeneration of the lifeworld of the traditional white working class. The bonding agent that held together these communities and made them work had been lost, and now things were disintegrating. The very stuff that had lent vitality to community life had somehow disappeared. Of course, they were not always morose, and they did not always spend their time complaining and discussing these issues with their peers. They were not so disgusted by Muslims that their disgust overshadowed their everyday lives. However, we had entered their lives to talk about the EDL and about their attitudes towards Muslims, and as soon as we raised these issues, things quickly changed. An amiable evening in the pub could quite quickly turn around as soon as immigration was raised as an issue for discussion.

Our conversations did not always hinge on angry racism, although, quite often, it was never very far away. Some spoke quite touchingly about their fears for future generations who, they believed, would have it even worse. They often spoke with great nostalgia for times past, and about their early lives surrounded by tough but principled proletarians who valued the stable community life that grew alongside England's modern industrial economy. For them, something was missing, and their communities were suffering immeasurably because of it. Many of our contacts connected the perceived downward mobility of their neighbourhoods to the loss of traditional forms of work and, up to a certain point, they were quite right about this. However, as we have seen, the next step was usually not to connect this loss of traditional forms of work and community to the neoliberal capitalist system, but to place the blame squarely on the arrival in England of huge numbers of immigrants. Their sadness at the loss of community cohesion quickly changed into anger at those they believed had caused this loss. In an important sense the psychological tension seemed to be caused by a contradiction of obedience – they were obeying the liberal establishment's traditional command to ignore the capitalist system as a causal mechanism, yet simultaneously disobeying its more recent command to embrace globalisation and multiculturalism.

Ultimately, they felt redundant, and this was especially true of our older respondents. It is certainly true that, as a class of men, they are of little practical use to Britain's high-tech, knowledge-based post-industrial market economy. Their skills are redundant and the world is rapidly passing them by. Some felt they belonged to a disappearing world. Their world had been a vibrant reality during their childhoods, but it was now fading into history. They often felt set apart from the new realities of 21st-century England. Their attitudes, beliefs and values didn't seem to fit anymore. Many couldn't see a way back. Those who were unemployed or underemployed often wanted traditional working-class jobs, but they also knew that these jobs had all but disappeared. They wanted to be producers. They wanted to work with their hands and apply their skills. But all of that was at an end.

David, who we spoke to at length, still hoped that that one day it might be possible for him to find his way into what remains of the region's productivist economy. However, in his more reflective moments, he also acknowledged that the chances of him making this transition were rapidly fading. He is not by any means an expert in macroeconomics, but he is smart enough to understand that it is cheaper for corporations to manufacture goods in low-wage economies in the east and the south. He takes no satisfaction whatsoever from his work as a security guard, and he is perpetually anxious about his financial situation. He is very keen to find regular employment. He doesn't want to become a burden on the state. David is understandably pessimistic about the future, and, in our view, he is, in a very basic sense, lashing out at those he has come to believe are responsible for his predicament.

Cut adrift from history, a traditional proletarian trapped in an environment in which traditional proletarian labour is almost entirely absent, David feels considerable anger at what has happened to his community, his class and himself. He feels short-changed. He wants to avail himself of all the indulgences of consumer culture, but instead he has to watch every penny just to make sure his family have enough food to eat and enough money to keep the heating on during winter. He has long brooded on these issues. He is not a stupid man. However, in channelling his aggression towards the Muslim community, he has failed to identify his true antagonist. The true cause of his frustration lies elsewhere.

FIVE

The hated 'centre'

All of our contacts expressed hatred for Muslim immigrants and radical Islamic terror groups. However, their deepest hatred was reserved for mainstream politicians. All mainstream politicians had abjectly and spectacularly failed. In fact, many of our contacts claimed that mainstream politicians had actively facilitated the degeneration of a once-great nation. They had capitulated to the EU and allowed immigrants to disturb what our respondents believed had been England's settled economy, national culture and regional variants. Politicians had made the British social security system a soft touch, and so prospective immigrants from all over the world were fighting hard to get into the country so that they could enrich themselves at the expense of white taxpayers. Politicians had enforced an illogical and unfair multiculturalism that subtly established a new range of injustices and antagonisms, and they displayed scant regard for the nation's history and culture. Chief among these new injustices was an institutionally and culturally legitimised prejudice against the heterosexual white working class.

The heterosexual white working class, our respondents believed, had been unfairly ascribed a broad range of regressive and illiberal characteristics, and they were now the only remaining cultural group without vocal political representation. Our respondents felt short-changed and used. They had been catapulted from the centre of English society and culture to the margins. England had been turned inside out, and politicians had actively assisted minority groups in this endeavour. Our contacts believed that politicians had been seduced by the image of 'the exotic'. They had grown to loath ordinary white working-class people. They wanted to appear cutting-edge, forward-looking, open, cosmopolitan and progressive. They wanted to embrace 'diversity' and cultural novelty, and the white working class was an uncomfortable reminder of times past. Ultimately, the career politicians of the centre-left and centre-right, keen to secure the liberal middle-class vote, wanted to forget the world the white working class represented. It's the future that counts, and the old proletariat didn't appear to figure prominently in the political class's visions of a go-getting, efficient, high-tech, business-friendly, cosmopolitan 21st-century Britain. Politicians wanted to forget the class system and industrial work cultures and reaffirm their commitment to a new global society built on openness, meritocracy, diversity and tolerance.

Our contacts believed that public policy now favoured minority sexualities, religions, ethnicities and lifestyles. They talked of occupational quota systems, and the drive to 'diversify' workforces. Newspapers and TV shows were full of talk about the problems faced by minorities, but they appeared totally blind to the problems faced by the white, heterosexual working-class population. The cultural mainstream, occupied by happily normal, everyday working people with no overriding religious or political commitments, appeared to have been forgotten. It existed only to be attacked as an oppressive force that bore down on those with marginally different social characteristics. In order for interest groups to draw support, they needed to separate themselves from this 'mainstream' and play up their credentials as victims. 'Normal' and 'ordinary' were quickly becoming terms of abuse. All the action had shifted to the outskirts. Gays, lesbians, ethnic minorities, transsexuals, the disabled.

For the most part our respondents were unconcerned about the presence of these groups in British civil society. Neither did they seem greatly concerned about Hindus, Jews or Afro-Caribbeans. Grand 'Jewish conspiracy' narratives, common among the pre-war far-right across Europe, were conspicuous only by their absence. We did not find particularly high levels of sexism or homophobia among supporters of the EDL – although some of the examples we did find could be extreme – and they certainly did not discriminate against the disabled. Despite the mass media's caricature of the EDL as a collection of atavistic and barbarous thugs, some of our contacts spoke in support of women's rights and they were quick to draw attention to what they believed to be the poor treatment of women and minorities in Islamic societies. Despite this, our contacts were, however, more than a little frustrated that the remaining population who did not fit into any of these categories had been ignored by those groups with the power to shape politics, economics and culture. They were even more upset by the supposed tendency of cultural elites to present white, working-class heterosexual men as some kind of oppressive social group that kept all of consumer society's glittering prizes for itself. That might be true for the upper class, but it certainly wasn't for them.

They felt totally ignored by mass-mediated culture. Gays, lesbians and ethnic minorities appeared to proliferate on television programmes and in other aspects of popular culture, but where were the authentic members of the white working class? They were always the thugs who grunted and threatened on the margins, and the ridiculous hammy caricatures that appeared on the soaps didn't count. And where were the working-class politicians? Our respondents couldn't identify a single one.

Some of our contacts were aware that the white working class was often lumped together with the white middle class, so that minorities could press their claim for better representation by positioning white natives as a homogenous and oppressive majority. In particular, they were aware that minorities often pointed to the elites of Westminster before claiming that white men were running the country. But which white men? The white men in Parliament had nothing whatsoever to do with our contacts. The differences were obvious for anyone willing to look beyond mere skin colour.

Our contacts were sure that they did not benefit from the fact white middle-class men still dominated in the main political parties. To lump the two groups together was totally nuts. Surely anyone with any sense could see that the posh middle-class public schoolboys of Westminster, who had attended elite universities and benefited from hidden but firmly established systems of patronage, had absolutely nothing to do with the white working class? It was idiotic to assume that political elites represented the interests of the white working class while ignoring the interests of minorities. In fact, our contacts believed that the opposite was the case. The state appeared determined to assist minorities and those born in other countries as much as possible, but it looked on the white working class with barely disguised contempt. Why couldn't other people see this? For our respondents, everyone else appeared to fare better than they did, and politicians were responsible for it all.

These ongoing political failures encouraged our respondents to believe that the entire Westminster system was corrupt. They despised mainstream politics, and they could see nothing at all of value in the staged theatrics of the party political system. On news broadcasts they did not see committed politicians keen to make Britain a better place, but shallow opportunists keen to capitalise on their elevated station. They could see politicians arguing with other politicians but, to our respondents, it was all a meaningless sham. These politicians didn't want to improve things. Not really. They just wanted to enrich themselves, achieve a degree of fame and prestige, and generally advance the interests of their preferred micro-community at the expense of everyone else.

For most of our contacts the political elites of Westminster were, in fact, the principal objects of hatred. These men reserved their most withering criticisms for politicians. Some of our sample presented Muslims as instrumental enemies keen to advance their own interests, and other immigrant groups were also disparaged on occasion. Our contacts were appalled by aspects of what they imagined to be Islamic culture and community life, and were willing to fight hard to overcome the growing strength of Islam in England.

However, paradoxically, they could, at a push, understand their opponents' dogged self-interest. They could understand the fight for enrichment and privilege. Underlying their racism was a deep and durable social Darwinism, the principle that it is a dog-eat-dog world and all are fair game, but they were simply unprepared to be passive losers. England's national culture had for many years evolved in a manner that reflected the economic imperatives of capitalism's competitive free market ideology. Muslims were simply determined competitors playing the game to the best of their ability, and there was nothing particularly mysterious or shocking about that. However, the politicians who encouraged and facilitated the advance of Muslim interests were deemed to have betrayed the nation. They had committed the ultimate crime of collaborating with the enemy and unilaterally disarming and disempowering the white working class in the midst of a competitive struggle.

The absurd and immovable commitment these politicians displayed to the vague categories of 'openness' and 'diversity' indicated quite clearly how divorced from the real world they had become. The trendy new language of multiculturalism, and the actual policies and political commitments that underpinned it, marginalised the very communities that during the 20th century had enabled the country to grow to become a genuine force on the world stage. The white working class were now dismissed as idiotic, slovenly and atavistic barbarians, while the true enemies of Great Britain were lauded as progressive creators of a new cultural positivity, beacons of vibrant and colourful diversity glowing with promise in the gloom that had fallen over post-industrial England.

These same politicians had weakened Britain's political system, besmirched its culture and established a new structural injustice that, under the cover of a barrage of meaningless liberal waffle about equality, fairness, respect and tolerance, established white working-class heterosexual men as the only cultural group that could be openly chastised, mocked and stigmatised. For our contacts, effete and cosseted metropolitan politicians, raised with the expectation that they would one day take up the mantle of their forebears and lead the country onwards, had trained their guns on the very men who had worked in industry, fought in wars, and generally made Britain one of the major superpowers of the 20th century. The country was eating itself. Everything was upside-down and inside-out. The heroes had become the villains, and the villains the heroes.

The abject failure of politicians didn't excuse Muslims. As we will see in the chapters that follow, to justify their negative hatred with positive reasons, our contacts believed they could identify in Muslim communities a broad range of barbaric behavioural traits. As we have already seen, the majority of our contacts did not classify themselves as racists. Instead, they believed that the

EDL and its supporters offered an entirely ethical and rational critique of England's Muslim community, and the religion of Islam more generally. Their aggression was justified in relation to a powerful and constant external threat that appeared totally relentless and hell-bent on establishing supremacy on behalf of Islam across the British Isles.

Our contacts were sure that representatives of this alien faith and culture were capable of unspeakable horror. They voiced this opinion often and many were quite knowledgeable about the activities of Islamic terror groups across Europe and further afield. They also knew details about the involvement of Muslim men in various crimes in English towns and cities. As we will see, grooming and the sexual exploitation of children inspired a visceral hated and a thirst for revenge, but our respondents were also avid collectors of factoids about the involvement of Muslim men in a range of other crimes.

Quite clearly, Muslims were already actively engaged in a battle to destroy English culture. They hoped to rip it to shreds and shatter the spirit of the English people so that they could begin the process of rebuilding the nation on a new foundation of Dark Age religious fundamentalism. All of this justified a guerrilla war that must be fought to determine the future of English cultural life. However, this simple justification was replete with the intersectional contradictions and absurdities that the recent shift from traditional politics to identity politics has brought upon us. Their Muslim antagonists were taking advantage of western liberalism in order to advance the most illiberal political, religious and cultural framework imaginable. Our contacts were angered by the stupidity of liberal elites, which flew in the face of reality to defend the rights of men totally dedicated to destroying human rights and establishing new systems of oppression.

They were shocked that western feminists denounced the EDL's politics as regressive, but felt comfortable defending a culture that appeared to tolerate the systematic subjugation and oppression of women across its territories. Why, they wondered, were so many of those in power unwilling to turn and look Muslim culture square in the face? Why were the EDL dismissed as barbarians when untold horrors had been perpetrated in the name of Islam, and by representatives of the Muslim faith? Why did the broad liberal left – often identified as 'cultural Marxists' by our contacts – tend to ignore forced marriages, the veiling of women, honour crimes, and the manifold evidence suggesting Muslim men were actively involved in the sexual exploitation of children? Why instead did they seek to demonise members of the white working class who were brave enough to speak up about the deeply problematic aspects of Muslim culture and community life? Radical Islamists had killed ordinary working people simply going about their business. Muslim paedophiles were preying on vulnerable children. They were turning previously functional areas into no-go zones that terrified the local white population. Muslims, our contacts believed, did not want to integrate. They abhorred English culture. Instead, they hoped to change English culture to suit their own preferences, and cared nothing at all about the lives of those who valued their own tradition and hoped to retain it at the core of their communities. If this trend continued, all would be lost.

The list of crimes placed at the door of Muslims was quite significant, and yet, our contacts believed, those in power inevitably and immediately rallied to their support. Even when discussing foreign wars, they positioned the British government as reserved, weak and half-hearted, following rules of warfare that were simply not recognised by their immoral fundamentalist adversaries. They pointed to acts of barbarous terrorism and the killing of ordinary people who had played no role in the oppression of Muslims and the advancement of western interests in the Middle East. This barbarism was the truth of Islam. The distinction between moderate and fundamentalist Muslims was simply a distraction. All Muslims, our contacts believed, were dedicated to the destruction of English culture and tradition. Islamic terrorism and the crimes of Muslims indicated a total lack of humanity at the core of Islam, and yet the west and its politicians appeared unwilling to take the forms of action needed to defeat such a dedicated opponent. And worse, Muslims continued to flood into Europe.

Our contacts felt they had been pushed into their current position. Generally speaking, they did not see themselves as fascists, and nor did they see themselves as particularly conservative or bigoted. Rather, they had taken to the streets only as a last resort. They were opposed to the fascism of Islamic doctrine, and they wanted those in power to take their concerns seriously. They would have liked to remain absorbed in their own work, private lives and idiosyncratic concerns, but they simply couldn't stand idly by and watch their culture besmirched any longer. They had identified a threat of huge significance, and they wanted others to wake from their slumber and look at the struggle that lay before them.

This was a fight of huge significance, and it was a fight they could not afford to lose. By standing with others who agreed, they had found a voice and a purpose. Standing together had given them the courage to press their case publicly. Their movement had no intellectual vanguard, and in truth there was no real sense of strategy or forward motion. They knew they didn't have all the answers; they just wanted to draw attention to the issues, express their dissatisfaction, and generally let it be known that they weren't going down without a fight. The goals they set for themselves and their movement were hazy and imprecise. It wasn't clear what success for the EDL would look like. But none of this mattered. They were doing it their way.

Accept our tutelage or be damned...

As we have seen, Muslims were identified as the new proximal enemy while the liberal middle class and their careerist politicians were identified as the distant systemic enemy, an anthropomorphic substitute for the hazily understood neoliberal system itself. This is the basic position. However, after many months of fieldwork we came to the conclusion that the hatred many of our respondents felt for mainstream politicians was really quite complex, and requires a careful and sustained analysis.

In particular, the hatred of the Westminster elite tended to bleed into a range of associated hatreds. Certainly, the nature of our respondents' critique of the generic 'liberal class' suggested an enmity that moved beyond simple economic pragmatism. Again and again they offered a vitriolic critique of a vaguely composed liberal middle class that, in their view, had accumulated significant power and then busied itself remaking England as a weird liberal dystopia composed of instrumental individuals and competitive, 'victimised' micro groups. Community obligations had been replaced by vapid consumerist individualism, and respect for established conventions and generations past was gone.

The fight for freedom from oppression had become the totem of 'progressive' politics. All concepts of universality had been abandoned. The new liberalism appeared to create a mood in which there could be no such thing as a just authority that might compel, control or punish the supposedly liberated and possessive postmodern subject. History, tradition, Christianity and the established rhythms of community life had been dismissed as stupid and regressive, and those who clung on to such concerns were simply repressed and fearful conservatives reluctant to move with the times. Nothing of value, it seemed, existed beyond the borders of liberal multiculturalism and its associated discourse of fairness, openness and equality.

For our contacts, representatives of this elite dominated all-important social institutions. They spoke at length of their hatred for soft, do-gooding hippies, liberals and multiculturalists. For them this vaguely composed group had won in the realm of politics and ideas, even though the real world was disintegrating. These hippies and do-gooders were judged to be representatives of the left. Generally speaking, our contacts knew very little about the history of the political left in England. They couldn't imagine that for most of its history the rank-and-file of 'the left' had been composed of everyday working-class men and women. However, because they had identified these hippies and do-gooders as enemies and collaborators, and because they appeared to occupy the position vacated by the traditional left, our contacts had decided that they were against 'the left' as such.

They talked of 'stupid lefties' who hated the working class. These 'stupid lefties' turned up at EDL protests to shout and spit at them and call them fascists. All of this encouraged our contacts to position themselves by a process of simple aversion on the political right, and they tended to understand their cause as a contemporary manifestation of a long-running antagonism between political opposites. They despised those committed to the myth of vibrant cosmopolitanism and cultural openness, and they were often staggered at what they imagined were the obvious paradoxes and contradictions of this discourse. They felt talked down to, patronised, and treated like dull-witted pupils who had failed to absorb the never-ending lesson on cultural tolerance.

Our contacts were angered that the 'liberal class' always placed itself in the didactic position of teacher. It was always the nice, supposedly warm-hearted philanthropic liberal who was entitled to deliver the sermon. This educated elite, pious and full of self-importance, but determined to present a magnanimous, open and thoughtful visage to the assembled throng, would instruct the great unwashed about the rules and regulations that pertain to a peaceful and tolerant 21st-century social life. It was the liberal class that told the working class how to live, what to believe in, and what to aspire to. It was the job of the white working class to listen intently and take notes in the hope of satisfying teacher that it was capable of playing nicely with the other kids, and abiding by the new rules of mutual toleration. The liberal class, as always, is, like the analyst, Lacan's 'one who is supposed to know'.

If the disorderly working class strayed beyond the boundaries of acceptable liberal thought and conduct they would be vigorously chastised. However, the liberal class always appeared capable of convincing itself that it did this in the interests of the working class. To clarify and solidify the utility of the lesson, studious pupils who had performed well would be plucked from the crowd and warmly congratulated. If these individuals continued to work hard they would progress. They must move away from their own histories to become something better. All they needed to do was embrace the supposedly progressive values of the metropolitan liberal middle class. If they could do this successfully, perhaps one day it would be they who delivered the lesson, although perhaps not from the highest pulpit.

Our contacts were, by this time, totally convinced that the liberal middle class was unwilling to take any direction from the working class. That wasn't how things worked. The working class was the recipient of the lesson, never its author. Even when members of the working class believed they had something vital to contribute — and our contacts believed their real-world experiences demanded attention — they were told to keep quiet and listen. Or worse, they would be allowed to speak, but they would not be listened to, and even when they were half-listened to, what they said would never be acted on. They would be smiled at and thanked, then patted on the head and told to retake their place among the audience. Nothing ever changed.

The core message of the new liberalism was that all cultural groups were equal, and all must be tolerated. However, our contacts could see no equality. Here were a bunch of metropolitan liberals – some of whom lived in big London houses and who sent their kids to private schools – telling men locked in insecure, declining, poorly paid and often degrading labour markets about equality. It was just a con, a trick to cover up their own piety and greed. The emphasis they placed on cultural equality was clearly connected to their absolute refusal to open discussions on the topic of economic equality. The saintly liberal class picked up decent salaries while their friends in the city made millions, and here they were, talking to hard-working men and women about equality.

Our contacts were sure that they had never been listened to. They were sure that for time immemorial their dissatisfactions had been studiously ignored by the self-appointed guardians of cultural propriety. Their lifetime was simply a continuation of this venerable tradition. Some of our respondents recalled past incidents in which they had been patronised and fobbed off by those they imagined to be representatives of this ruling liberal class. One had heard his father talk about a deputation of steelworkers from County Durham who had travelled to London in 1980 to protest about the closure of their steelworks, but not a single MP came out to talk to them. Inevitably, they felt angry, frustrated and ill-used.

If the working class had something important to say, it could do so only by ticking a box on a ballot paper at election time. That had to suffice. Any attempt to move beyond this framework would be judged to be threatening and illegal. Listen carefully and abide by the rules. Do as you're told, toe the line, and everything will work out swimmingly.

Our contacts concluded that all this talk of openness, freedom and toleration was bollocks. It was the same with equality. It was just a front used to disguise darker motivations. Our contacts certainly didn't feel themselves to be recipients of a new-found freedom. In fact, they experienced a palpable lack of freedom. They felt hemmed in, controlled, and often quite desperate and angry. They felt pressurised, and thwarted at every turn. Certainly, there was little freedom to be found in competitive labour markets with very low rates of pay. Where was the freedom for the retail worker struggling by on a zero-hours contract? Where was the freedom for the underemployed security guard anxious about turning on the heating? Where was the freedom for the tradesman struggling to keep his head above water in an already shrinking and desperately competitive marketplace?

There was little freedom when money was tight, and threats, real and imagined, lay around every corner. And exactly where was this choice they heard so much about? They didn't choose to be downwardly mobile. They didn't choose to see their communities disintegrate, and they didn't choose to be surrounded by wave after wave of new economic competitors. They didn't choose multiculturalism, and they didn't choose to see Muslim interests advance year on year. But here they were. Ultimately, they felt box-pressed, shut in, forced on to an increasingly narrow and disintegrating peninsula from which things of real value were rapidly disappearing from view as the sea-level rose around them. There were huge expanses of popular consumer culture that our contacts either couldn't understand or couldn't access. Freedom, like equality and everything else these liberals droned on about, repeating their tired mantra over and over again, was ultimately a load of shit. It meant nothing, and it meant nothing because it was nothing.

When our contacts were together – online, in the pub, at the football match, and especially at one of their demonstrations – they felt constantly surveilled and inconvenienced by the forces of law and order, and by their political opponents on the left. While demonstrating in towns and cities across the country they were shouted at, spat at, and assaulted. Some had been quite badly injured by missiles and police batons. Many were fearful that they would be identified as supporters of the EDL, and would lose their jobs as a result. Tolerance, it seemed, didn't extend to their peculiar version of postmodern nationalism. And where was their freedom of speech? Even the radical Muslim clerics who spouted hate and advocated violence appeared to do better on this front. In an era of supported tolerance and diversity, the powerful had quite clearly decided that the views of EDL supporters should not be tolerated. Apparently, the EDL's political project was just too different. It appeared that diversity was a good thing, but only within the ill-defined limits set by metropolitan liberal elites. Their intolerance would not be tolerated. However, it seemed that the intolerance of Islamic extremists and their middle-class liberal supporters would be tolerated, no matter how extreme.

Our contacts felt that they were expected to discard their communities and family backgrounds and recreate themselves as upwardly mobile and instrumental consumers, keen to engage with the new and invigorating opportunities opening up on the field of culture. To them, the new freedom they heard so much about was actually a life of quiet submission and acquiescence, a life in which the individual must accept the disintegration and disappearance of all traditional cultures before jumping headlong into an ocean of insubstantial consumer toss and smiley liberal optimism. As far as we could see in our interviews, the truth was that they didn't want to leave their communities behind to engage in a remorseless battle for upward mobility. They didn't want to recreate themselves as happy corporate automatons in order to be granted access to the middle echelons of the service economy.

Some felt sure that they were subject to systematised negative discrimination. Others only went as far as to suggest that they had been completely forgotten. Often they felt over-policed, marginalised and despised. They believed themselves to be simply speaking out for those who were worried and angry about the way things were going. They knew others out there felt the same but were too scared to make their feelings known. They believed they spoke on behalf of a great many others, and they hoped their presence on the political stage would encourage others to join them. Soon, they hoped, it would become clear that the British people had had enough. Politicians would be forced to listen.

They didn't always appear depressed, angry and disengaged, but they were sure that, for them, there was little to feel genuinely optimistic about. Things were getting worse, and they had been getting worse for a while. In a world obsessed with freedom and openness, they wanted certainty and security. They wanted to return to the established rhythms of an English life they believed they had once known. They wanted functional social institutions, comprehensible biographical paths, functional identities and a reasonably fixed and secure system of entitlements and obligations. Ultimately, they wanted something to believe in. They wanted something real they could rely on. They wanted their own cultural norms and experiences to be validated and rendered meaningful, rather than washed away in furtherance of a project that offered only vague platitudes about progress, openness and freedom. Why were their experiences dismissed as meaningless? Who had decided that the disintegration of working-class community life was a price worth paying in exchange for the insubstantial benefits of this new open society?

The discourse of reflexive postmodern liberalism encourages us all to believe that we are the architects of our own lives, identities and biographies. We can, apparently, transform ourselves and our society at a whim. However, our contacts reacted in opposition to these supposedly reflexive and transformative freedoms. What we see here represented by our contacts' anger is not a fundamental distinction between the supposed faith and commitment of modernism and the cynicism and liberalism of the postmodern epoch. Rather, these two modes of social organisation are two sides of the same coin. They exist in tandem. For example, when, during the era of really existing socialism, dissident movements arose in Eastern Europe to demand new freedoms, such groups structured their demands in relation to the perceived 'totalitarianism' of the existing sociopolitical order. The same is true with the EDL, only in reverse. Now, in an era of panoramic freedom and liberal relativism, we are seeing new 'dissident' movements arise that seek to dispel the insubstantiality of postmodernism in the hope of establishing new fixed structures and objects of truth that might provide them with a degree of security in troubled times. The drive to create new freedoms is connected dialectically to the drive to create new forms of security, certainty and belief. Because neither system is on its own capable of providing a secure platform for a satisfying life, the dominance of one facilitates the drive to create the other.

Certainly, our contacts bristled at the liberalisation and deconstruction of everything that had once seemed solid, steadfast and dependable. Behind the public Islamophobia lay a general desire to return to a world in which everything immediately made sense, and where they felt valued and at home. They wanted everyone to respect the nation and its traditional culture, because, they were sure, it had once been worthy of respect, and it could be again. However, it now seemed that immigrants, who appeared to have benefited greatly from the country's largesse, wanted to mock all of this, and sections of the white middle class were happy to join them. These groups found the national flag, the national anthem, the royal family, and the more earthy aspects of common culture, to be ultimately regressive.

Soft power, hard power

Glaring flaws pervade the EDL's narrative, which we will return to later. However, in the meantime, we should keep in mind that our contacts are, overwhelmingly, working-class men with minimal education. Their discourse developed entirely in the absence of an informed vanguard. Of course, this doesn't mean that their narrative can be simply dismissed as stupid and irrelevant. Rather, we must seek to understand this narrative. We must understand where it comes from, why Muslims in particular are demonised, and why the dissatisfactions of these men have not been dealt with by the contemporary liberal democratic system. What can the anger of EDL supporters and the kernel of truth that exists at the core of their unaffected discourse tell us about contemporary England and the problems it faces?

According to Big Waz:

> 'I tell you who I hate, right: fucking Muslims and suicide bombers, fucking paedophiles and rapists. Fucking ISIS-supporting jihadi-types who want to fucking destroy this country. Fucking hippies and weirdos and socialists, in fact anyone who calls us fascists and doesn't give a fuck about the working

class. Fucking politicians with their fingers in the till. All of them.'

Although most of their ire is reserved for the liberal left, the EDL hate the middle class in general – the politicians, journalists, academics, and everyone else connected to the privileged, salaried and relatively secure middle-class elite that appears to be running things. This elite seems to have seized power in a quiet revolution. They are the masters of soft power, and peddlers of influence in politics, culture and the economy. According to our contacts, since its ascent to power, this vaguely defined group had been engaged in the task of advantaging their multiethnic friends and transforming England to suit their own cultural and political preferences. They seemed to be inspired by a vision of a future England in which all religions and all ethnic groups would forget both new and traditional animosities to forge a positive new culture of tolerance that would disguise and compensate for the inevitable and increasingly stark injustices of a thoroughly liberalised and unforgivingly competitive economy. The middle-class liberals' ultimate failure lies in their constant denial of the fact that in this crucible of competition it will take an awful lot more than an attempt to socially engineer multicultural tolerance to ensure a peaceful future.

For our respondents, behind all the talk of openness and equality lay stupidity, ignorance, naivety, cowardice, duplicity and class prejudice. This elite quite clearly found the white heterosexual working class uncouth and regressive. Yet the elite's political weakness had allowed the forces of global neoliberalism to destroy traditional labour markets, rip apart white working-class communities and abruptly reduce the status and security of the traditional white working class. Despite their educational qualifications and their confident oratory, their actions had been myopic, incompetent and socially catastrophic. To cap it all, our contacts emphasised, they had the temerity to advocate the rights of immigrants while palpably failing to ensure the continuing security and modest lifestyles of the working class. To our contacts, this elite appears to be fucking things up on a monumental scale.

Steppy is 39. He has supported the EDL for many years. Most of his activism takes place on the internet, and he is a regular contributor to various comment sites. Steppy claims to be a voracious reader. He certainly seems to have absorbed some of the more populist literature on contemporary Islamic terrorism, and he displays some awareness of ongoing political tensions in the Middle East. He is not a violent man, and eschews the violence that seems to typify EDL protests. Generally, he spoke calmly, but his anger was real:

Steppy: 'Look, people should know what's going on. It's serious, deadly serious. People don't realise. On the surface it all looks nice and friendly but underneath it's a nasty thing. It's taking us backwards. We're behind the French, the Germans, everyone. We're the poor man of Europe now. We used to have an Empire, for fuck's sake. Now look.'

Interviewer: 'What are you talking about?'

Steppy: 'These posh white people. They're not your usual aristocrats. They're more like really privileged, stuck-up public schoolboys. They've taken over the Labour Party. They're taking over everywhere. And look what they're doing. First thing, they get their mates top jobs. And then their mates get jobs for their mates. Your feminists are cut from the same cloth. They talk about democracy, but there's no democracy. Not in this country. You've got people in Labour and the Conservatives that used to go to school together. They went to university together, lots of them. Then you find out that the news reporters and all the people on TV actually know each other, know the politicians: their kids go to the same schools, stuff like that. It's just a stitch-up mate. They act like they're at each other's throats but secretly they agree because they're all pals. They're all went to posh schools on their Daddy's money. Posh little spoilt cunts who've never had to work for anything.

'And look what happens. They've got no idea what it's like around here. They think everyone's a fucking vegan and shops at Waitrose. They think everyone sends their kids to university and goes on holiday to Morocco, or wherever they go. They want everyone to be nice to each other, be nice to criminals and murders and paedophiles, be nice to terrorists who want to bomb us and kill us. Don't say anything bad about Muslims, no matter what you do, because that's racist, right? So we've got to be polite to Muslims who want to get rid of our laws. They do. They say we should take our laws from the Koran. And they want us to just go along with it, even though, up until about 20 years ago, there's been no Muslims here, and we've been a Christian country for centuries and centuries... They say it's a good thing, and we should just say "okay", and let them all come over, let them all claim benefits, bring their families over, let everybody in.

'We should say nothing, right, if they want to stand on our streets and tell everyone we're all infidels, say there should be a holy war to wipe out all non-believers... I'm not kidding. Look at the drugs, the crime, the paedos, the gangs of [Muslim] lads they've got running about now, saying white people aren't allowed to go through their areas... It wouldn't have happened 30, 40 years ago, would it? The people wouldn't stand for it, and neither would the politicians back then. Now there's nothing. And it's all because these bastards are running the show, isn't it? "Diversity" and "tolerate this" and "tolerate that", they do my fucking head in mate.'

Anth is 27. He offers a similar story. He is particularly keen to discuss what he sees as the paradoxes and contradictions of multiculturalism and other aspects of left-liberal discourse:

'These fucking stupid cultural Marxist cunts, they seem to think everything is the fault of us. It's western imperialism to blame, it's western oppression and racism to blame. 9/11 and 7/7, we should prostrate ourselves on the floor because we're guilty. They don't look at the Islamist ideology, the drive for domination globally. Muslim fucking superiority is the issue.

'Afro-Caribbeans, Sikhs, Hindus, Jews, they integrate into British society. Muslims don't. They want to fucking come here. That isn't the damage of the Empire. That's the good it did. It isn't racism. The racism is hating Great Britain, and it's the cultural leftists that hate Britain. That's why they're happy for Muslims to piss all over British values. None of those other groups do, do they? None of those other groups are blowing up trains. It's fucking Muslims, that's what the problem is.

'ANTIFA [the Anti-Fascist Network] are the worst of the lefties. I mean most of them are fucking wet as, but they have some decent types that will have it [he means, who will have a fight]. But if you look at most of those who oppose us, most of the lefties, they are fucking gangly ginger-haired fucking animal rights-supporting vegans that fucking want Muslims to have the freedom to eat Halal meat! They are the fucking man-hating feminists with faces full of metal piercings that oppose patriarchy, but they're defending Islamic FGM [Female Genital Mutilation] and the Sharia idea of the women being half of a man. I mean, seriously, I just want to know what it is that makes them so fucking stupid. I mean a lot is brainwashing in universities, you can see it.

'They say we're racists, so we can't have them
marching on our streets. We can't be liberal about it
and let the EDL just demonstrate and be heard. But
then, if you tried asking them what they're all about,
why are they're opposing us, why are they coming
onto the streets, and they're like, "we are defending
liberal, multicultural society, no one can challenge
that!" You see, how fucked up is that?'

Anth, in a similar way to others we spoke to, believes that
these various left-liberal groups are part of a vaguely coherent
political and cultural establishment that sets down firm rules on
the parameters of acceptable political activity. For Anth, they
are perhaps not the dominant group, but they certainly form
part of an elite that believes itself to be so enlightened that it
can instruct the working class on what is and is not achievable
on the field of politics. Anth believes that he sees through the
whole charade. Ultimately, for him, these various groups are
composed of middle-class liberals who have been conned into
believing that Islam is a progressive religion that has a great deal
to contribute to contemporary English cultural life.

Barry is 39. Like Anth and Steppy, he does not conform to the
usual EDL stereotype. He has attended only one street protest,
and he hopes the EDL can now begin to adapt its strategies in
order to appeal to a broader demographic. Again, like Anth
and Steppy, he is reasonably knowledgeable about 20th-century
English history and some aspects of contemporary geopolitical
contestation. He maintains that the various groups who oppose
the EDL, and form counter-demonstrations at EDL street
protests, in fact cause most of the problems:

'UAF [United Against Fascism] are the ones
campaigning to ban our marches. They all call us
fascists, but who can't handle a different view? When
are we saying they should be banned? It's the SWP
[Socialist Workers Party] and UAF that are the violent
ones. I'm real in saying that 90% of the trouble that's
caused at our demonstrations comes from them.
They're violent and want to drive us off the streets

because they don't like that we're angry. And yet we're the fascists. Can you explain that one, because I can't? They think we're uneducated, we can't read books, but the problem is they're all middle-class sorts indoctrinated into cultural Marxist political ideology in university, so the things they should read, they don't.

'How are these SWP lefties supporting what's going on now with this Muslim immigration? Do they not know if it happens and they all get into Europe the white race will be wiped out by 2050, huge decline by 2030? It's a fact. If you go and do real research you'll see that it's unavoidable if we let any more in. It's not racist to keep the white race alive. It's not racist to be proud of our white Christian heritage and the country we had. I want that country back, and its sorts like them that sent it to the fucking dogs.'

Big Bruce is 43 and much more comfortable with physical confrontation. He is a friend of Paul and David's, who we met in the last chapter, and he has an established reputation for violence:

'UAF? I could beat the lot of them with one hand tied behind my back. Honest, all of them groups, all of them, they're fuck all, just fuck all mate. Most of them are fucking lesbians and spotty faced kids who've got no idea what more Muslims in this country means. They shout a lot but they're just fucking cowards. I'd love it, just one time, [if] the police fucked off and left us to it. Oh, that would be it for me. I'd eat the lot of them. They're fucking toe-rags, absolute cunts. They stand there dressed like tramps, shouting their mouth off... Honestly, I can't stand them. To me, they're what's wrong with this country. I see them with their fucking banners and I just despair. If it's them we are supposed to be like we may as well give up now, you know, let the Muslims take over and start raping kids and stoning people to death.

'You just look at them and you think, everything is just upside down. These are supposed to be good people, right, people we're all supposed to follow and listen to? Honest, I just despair. Who are these people? I can't understand it. I get so angry about it. I bring my kids up to be proper men. I bring them up to stand up for their mates. I tell them to look out for each other, do the right thing. I can't really explain. They're just like the politicians: fucking smarmy, smiley do-gooders who're just out for number one. To me, they're just the fucking worst, they are.'

Interviewer: 'To you they're worse than Muslims?'

Big Bruce: 'Difficult one, but yes, they're worse. They're sticking up for these people when really they've got no idea what they're sticking up for. They think we're bullies but it's them that's bullies. They couldn't give a fuck about the likes of us. When we say immigrants are taking over our cities they tell us to shut up and stop complaining. These posh cunts, these fucking university people, they tell us we've got to go along with it. They say it's us what's causing problems. Unbelievable. It's too much for me sometimes, coz they don't have to put up with the shit we have to put up with. They don't see it. Or maybe they do and they don't care, I don't know. But I hate them. They're so, what's the word, full of themselves, something like that. They're so sure they're right and that there's no problem with more Muslims. Let them all in, they say, they're doing no harm. And behind them I can see the Muslims grinning. Because already you see the problems. And it's going to get worse. No doubt really is there? These fucking stupid lefties, I wish they could see the brothels springing up, all Asian owned, the crime, the drugs, the problems what's happening all over the place. You see them defending paedophiles on TV, saying it's racist to say anything about it. I mean, these are people that are hacking up Lee Rigby [a soldier killed by Islamic extremists in London in 2013]. They're killing ordinary people on their way to work. They're mass murdering over in France. But it's the fucking EDL what's the bad guys, right?'

Paul, who we met in the last chapter, has not been active in the EDL, but he has considerable charisma. When he speaks he commands the attention of his friends and acquaintances. He has this to say:

'The politicians that's running things, you see it on the news and you see how much they've just fucked things up monumentally. The debt, the country's in that much debt, the number can't even be counted, it's growing so quickly. Soon there'll be nowhere else to go and the whole thing will collapse. And to be honest, I couldn't care. Let it collapse. People have got to understand what these people [the politicians] have done. Years and years of history down the pan. But I couldn't care anymore to be honest. Let it happen… in the end people will see what's happened, and they'll see we were right all along.

'They've [politicians] given millions away to their pals, haven't they? Millions. They've wasted so much money it's unbelievable. Banks and foreign charities and aid and then all the money they've given away in dole money and council houses and everything. They've just got no respect: no respect for the country, no respect for the people.

'It's not just around here. People all over the place are just starting to wake up to what's happened. See, people don't say anything till it's them losing their jobs, till it's them with their kids in bother, till a mosque pops up on the corner of their street and loads of Pakis are swanning about all over the place. Wait until a bunch of Polish move in next to you and they're up all night drinking and shitting in the street. Wait till it's your kids getting beaten up by gangs of Pakis walking to school. It's not just, it's happened. It's been allowed to happen. They [the politicians] wanted all of this to happen.'

Colin is 36 and has been reasonably active in the EDL for around eight years:

'A lot of the UAF, they're fucking stupid apologists for the history of England and Wales from the 1700s. It's like we should feel guilty about the British Empire because it was evil, it raped and pillaged, that sort of fucking shite. No mention of how it spread fucking enlightened attitudes, of how our industrialism advanced and improved the world. They genuinely seem to think we should be ashamed of the industrial, enlightened history that we spread. That's fucking mental. I wasn't responsible for fucking slavery. I didn't fucking benefit! Lots of fucking MPs, their ancestors did. Mine would've been fucking hauling coal, would've been more like the slave than a slave owner.'

Big Jim is 49. He has never attended an EDL rally, but he is a staunch advocate of the EDL's anti-Muslim discourse:

'Everything in this country is getting more fucked up, more stupid. I can't see why we need to say we aren't anti-Muslim. There isn't much difference to me between the bloody moderate and an extremist Muslim, there really isn't. Look, because, in truth, the Koran tells the moderates that they should seek to live under Sharia. They want the Halal meat, they want women veiled, they want no alcohol, more mosques. They're all intolerant of Jews and gays. But then, this is what gets me, you have fucking liberals who're, on one hand, all about the ethical treatment of fucking animals, wouldn't wear fur, buy farm-assured meat and RSPCA-branded chickens, but they say Halal meat is okay. Fucking stupid liberal fucking feminists, who are into women's rights, saying the burka is a choice, or FGM is just the same as male circumcision. What the fuck! They're defending fucking Islamists who hate them! These fucking idiots, mate, these fucking commie fucking liberal idiots, they need fucking hanging.'

Jake, 45, continues with this theme:

Jake: 'If you are working class, white and patriotic you are seen as scum. The people in power and the middle class are ashamed to call themselves English. If you listen to them, they expect you to self-identify as British, liberal and fucking tolerant. If you call yourself an English Nationalist, some people see that as a provocation and a badge you're racist and intolerant.'

Interviewer: 'What does that mean to you then, English Nationalist?'

Jake: 'I'm English; I see England as my country, not Scotland… or Wales. I am pro-Union, but I am not British like the fucking BNP. I would never vote for them because I'm not British, I'm English. I don't follow the British football team. I believe in keeping English jobs for English people first, and I am not a fucking liberal. I am fucking intolerant of some things, like fucking Sharia law and fucking child brides. Those are fucking things I should be fucking intolerant of, and I don't fucking want them in my country. It's a bloody good job the previous generations were intolerant of some things too. If the previous generations were not intolerant of Nazism we would have the swastika as a flag now.'

Kenny is 45. He is not a particularly dedicated supporter of the EDL, but he hates mainstream politicians, and he believes absolutely that the arrival of millions of Muslims has disrupted English culture and community life:

> 'It all started with the fucking politicians, mate, I would shoot them with all the scum Muslims. The Conservatives never gave a fuck coz they know they don't have to live with dirty Muslims in their big London houses, but Labour, they're worse. I remember Labour sticking up for blacks, and that was fair enough because they [black people] came here and got on with it, they didn't rock the boat... but Labour didn't give a fuck when the Muslims came in and started taking the piss. They did nothing. They should have capped immigration, they should have protected the working class, but those cunts, they opened the floodgates. I don't like the BNP. I'm not racist. But immigration now, it's Muslim immigration: Somalia, Iran, Iraq, Afghanistan, Pakistan, that is where they are coming from... The EDL basically, well, they are willing to tell these Muslims we have had enough of them. It's that, basically. If they can't live with us then get out, go back to wherever, you know?'

Richy has been arrested many times. He has been charged with various racially motivated crimes, and appears sanguine at the prospect of eventual imprisonment. Here he describes what drew him to the EDL:

> 'They can arrest me, lock me up, I don't give a fuck. The first demo I went to was in Manchester. It was great: it was on the news and we couldn't be ignored anymore. It was kicking off that got people to notice. The media and the politicians hate the working class like me... They don't say what we think about these fucking immigrants. No one gives a fuck about the working class. This country was built on the back of people like us, hardworking working-class people, and no one's sticking up for us.

'I didn't like the BNP because I'm not a racist, I don't buy into their views. I don't mind people with skills coming in, but I don't want an open door and I don't want to be told what I can and can't think and say. The EDL, when they started out, look at what they were against: fucking "grooming" and paedophiles, Sharia law in our fucking country and a fucking creeping multiculturalism that loved and welcomed anybody and everybody except the working-class white, Protestant, straight man. Well fuck it, I didn't want to be silenced anymore, and if I have to have a row with some coppers and have a row to get my voice heard, then bring it on.'

Damien is 22. He has attended EDL rallies, and he remains a determined advocate of their anti-Muslim discourse. Here he expresses views common to our overall sample:

'I fucking don't really get politics mate, left and right. I'm not a racist, I have mates who are black, I grew up with black people round me, but they fitted in with us, we got along together, in and out of each other's houses. It's not like that today. That community feeling, it's gone. I don't know, just like, I know everyone calls the EDL far right, so that is what I guess I am, fair enough. All I know is that I fucking hate those who oppose us, the fucking UAF and the fucking cultural Marxists. They are just queers, dirty spoilt whores who like ethnic cock, and middle-class pricks that don't know what life is really like when you live on a shitty fucking estate where everything is disappearing except the fucking foreign faces.'

We met David in the last chapter. Here he expands on the reasons why he supports the EDL:

'The Labour Party round here have been no end of bother. It's them that's caused it as far as I'm concerned. They're the one's that's started it all by letting them [Muslim immigrants] all in. I get pissed off about it because people around here still vote Labour. Drives me around the bend. Why would you do that? Keep voting for the ones who've destroyed this whole area? You've got people voting Labour who haven't had a job for years and years. You've got people voting Labour when their kids can't get jobs, when the schools are a mess, when the fucking NHS is falling apart, everything's going wrong, right? These are the people that's responsible, and you're still voting for them? The Labour Party now's got nothing to do with working people, but working people still vote for them. These people are fucking idiots. They're being led about by the nose. They just can't think for themselves… I'm just disgusted by them all mate, all of them, all politicians, the local, the national, the lot. I wouldn't trust any of them. They're thieves. They're bleeding the country dry. They just grab what they can and then, when they kicked out, the other lot start robbing everyone blind. They're one and the same to me. There's no difference. Just a bunch of soft southern cunts grabbing what they can [and] making sure all their mates are all right.

'You can just tell how corrupt everything is, the state the economy's in. Underneath all that multicultural bullshit is just their thieving. It's just all bollocks. They try and put a spin on it but you'd have to be stupid not to know that everything is totally fucked… They're carving up the country is the truth of it. Everyone's out for themselves, everyone's got their hand out. The rich want more, the Asians want more, the fucking Scottish want more, the Welsh, the Jews, the blacks, the whites, it's just the same thing over and over. The country has been run down, for years it's been going on. There's nothing left from what I can see.

'And then they point at me and say I'm the bad guy. I'm the bad guy when all I want to do is stick up for this country. All I want is for a bit of respect for our history and our traditions, a bit of respect for the white people who sweated their balls off building this country... Being a Christian now, being white and straight, working for a living, that's seen as a bad thing, isn't it? Be honest. All your university people fucking hate the likes of us. They'd shit themselves if they were sitting here wouldn't they? That's it, just forget about us, isn't it?

'They want to ban the bomb, hug a hoody, all that other fucking lefty bollocks. They don't know what world we're living in... Look, there's people in this pub who haven't got a pot to piss in, and they've come here because they want to stick up for this country. We're right mate. We are the ones who're right. They can slag us off as much as they want, it doesn't really matter anymore.'

Big Waz is a friend of Big Bruce. He had a difficult start to life and he was in trouble with the police for much of his youth. In recent years he has sold cannabis and marijuana and become involved in other forms of illicit trading to supplement either welfare payments or low wages. He has this to say:

'The young ones can't get a job. The place is a tip. There's no money for anything. The council's cutting back, everything's cutting back. The world is going to shit mate, simple as. I'm trying to get my mam moved, because where she lives now, it's just not right. I went up there, and on the stairs, right, there's piss and rubbish and drug stuff scattered about. Honestly, I've been up there loads of times, I've been on at people to fix it... You've got heroin up there, and you never saw heroin when I was a boy. And I know where it's coming from. It's Asians what are bringing it into the country. You've got Asians now, gangs of them, and what do they care if the place turns to shite? It's jihad, it's what they call jihad. They want to bring the drugs in to fuck things up for the local people. They want addicts, right? Addicts are good for business. It's about money, but if they can kill off a few white people too, then great, that's their attitude.

'The school has had trouble with gangs, gangs of Asians. They've got their brothers, older kids, hanging around outside robbing the young lads going in. There's been fights, gang fights, cars have been smashed up, then you've got more and more people carrying knives. You're seeing stabbings now. It's got to the stage where there's got to be some organisation, just to make sure that the kids can get into school safe. See, to me, these are things your politicians should be dealing with. That's their job as far as I can see, but what ever gets done? My mam's got to come out of that flat and walk through piss and shit and fuck knows what all over the stairs. There's kids outside getting pissed at all hours. You've got, loads and loads of people hanging around because no one's got work the next morning, right? All kinds of drugs there is now, young kids I'm talking about, things I know nothing about. And I can't find anyone to give a shit. No one.'

We met Young Bren earlier. He says:

'It's not having money mate, that's what pisses me off. I need some new gear. I'm sick of bumming drinks off people… I'd don't want to talk about all that politics stuff mate. I don't understand it and it just does my head in. I'm just sick really. I'm a good lad but there's just fuck all, and more and more I just hate it, the way things are going. It's shit and it never used to be like that I don't think.

'Mostly I just go [to EDL rallies] because there's nowt else to do, and if some of the lads are going. It pisses me off coz there's Pakis all over the place and all of them's got better gear than me, cars and that. That's just not right is it? There's Pakis around here that are proper flash but they're just robbing the system. They've got houses crammed full of people and the place, well, it's not what it was. It's the same with the Europeans and the Gypos.

'You hear them [his friends] talking, and it makes sense, but I don't understand a lot of it. They're saying we've been had over, that they're all coming over here and there's not enough to go around, not enough jobs, not enough houses. I can't see why we let them in when they're bombing us. Did you see about that Lee Rigby? That's what it's like. There are fights all the time around here but you never hear about it. One day it'll happen here for real. And look what kind of people they are. They've already got gangs in the school and that.

'I can't be bothered, really. I don't know. I'm like them [his friends], just sick of being treated like shit. Just angry. It just fucks me off, everything about it. They get right on my nerves. They're lefties aren't they, the ones who turn up to shout [at EDL rallies]? They do my head in totally mate. They're shouting at me, but all we're saying is we should kick out the Muzzies coz they hate us. All we're saying is it's not right, the rapes and the murders and the bombs and that. We just want to defend the country, but everyone's against us. It's mad. They stick up for people who are cutting people's heads off and fucking kids, but we're like, the worst, that's what they think.'

Racist multiculturalism

As we have seen, all our contacts were opposed to the ideology of multiculturalism. Their core suggestion was that a liberal dogma had established itself at the core of English society. They were keen to be understood on this point. This liberal dogma actively sought to crush all alternative viewpoints, but it did so by stealth. It presented itself as open and tolerant, but underneath this appealing veneer lay new forms of intolerance, and good old-fashioned economic self-interest. For our contacts, the supposed 'openness' of contemporary culture was a myth. There was no mixing of cultures. Not really. Their experience suggested separatism and conflict had been the outcome of this particular experiment, and this was especially true with regard to Muslims. The presumed refusal of Muslims to assimilate set them apart, and this refusal, it was argued, contributed to the rapid growth of anti-Muslim feeling among neighbour members of the white working class. Some of our contacts wanted to stress the importance of retaining the cultures and traditions of the white working class, but this was not the whole story. It is worth delving a little deeper into their critique of multiculturalism.

Why is it considered reasonable, even essential, to dispense with a traditional culture in order to establish a new multicultural configuration in its place? This question arose again and again over the course of our study. Many of our contacts failed to see anything particularly great about 'diversity' and the mixing of cultures, yet, oddly, they were also aware that many groups had been happy to integrate into English culture and accept its values. Rather, the problem lay with the religion of Islam specifically. Muslims didn't want to integrate, and this, according to our contacts, is where the logic of multiculturalism began to break down. Our contacts were not against multiculturalism in principle, but they were certainly against the specific model of multiculturalism imposed on them by the unworldly and incompetent liberal class in denial of the consequences of their failed model.

Unlike the liberal class, many of our contacts were aware of the real division between the economic and cultural spheres. Many spoke passionately about falling wages and growing competition for jobs. Many complained about recently arrived immigrants working cash-in-hand for rates below the minimum wage. As we will see in the next chapter, there was also a great deal of discussion about the perceived economic successes of Muslims. Underneath a thin veneer of cultural positivity, multiculturalism had encouraged ferocious economic competition and a great deal of anxiety about what the future may hold. The liberal class, safe in their highly capitalised social networks and salaried occupations, float above this brutal economic competition, and have no real experience of it.

Some of our contacts had seen representatives of the liberal class on television talking about the great benefits immigration had brought to the economy. These liberals, we were told, talked about growing competition, falling wages and increasing corporate profits without any consideration of the problems faced by people forced to find work in the low-wage service sector. They understood the formal economy only as an abstraction. They couldn't even imagine the millions of working people desperate to earn enough cash to sustain themselves and their families. They couldn't imagine the pressure involved. Big Baz had this to say:

> 'I saw it on TV the other night, right. There's this bloke talking about immigrants, and how we should have more because the economy gets stronger. Unbelievable. He's got these graphs and everything, and he's talking about competition, this, that and the other, and how there needs to be more profits so companies get stronger. Unbelievable. I want to see that cunt deal with fucking Europeans coming over, saying they'll do his job for half the price. Fucking wanker. I want to see that cunt when it's his kids can't get jobs. Immigrants good for the economy? It's just all lies. It's just cunts like him looking to make money out of it. Let him deal with the shit I have to deal with, and then we'll see if immigrants are a good thing.'

Big Baz's knowledge of macroeconomic processes is not particularly advanced, but it is worth pausing for a moment to appraise the connections between the cultural and economic spheres in a little more detail. Multiculturalism, quite clearly, forms part of the ruling ideology today. It offers a positive cultural programme to sit alongside a negative economic programme in which we continue to see the brutal reallocation of money and resources from mainstream civil society to the plutocrats who sit at the top of our national and international economies. The progressive mixing of populations and the supposed diversity of our culture is not at all antagonistic to neoliberalism. We should keep in mind that the gap between rich and poor is now wider than it was during *La Belle Époque*, the previous bourgeois heyday of the capitalist project. In the new bourgeois heyday, the growth of multiculturalism has neither prevented nor even slowed down the relentless widening and deepening of economic inequality, or the hardships faced by millions trapped at the bottom of civil society.

It should strike us as odd that today so many on the left believe that the fundamental problems we face relate to an absence of tolerance and cultural acceptance rather than an absence of equality and economic inclusion. Why has so much emphasis been placed on tolerating diversity and the creation of a just cultural order when so little emphasis has been placed on the creation of the just economic order we need to accommodate it? While it would be unfair to say that all on the left have abandoned the traditional leftist project of structural change, quite clearly, interest in economic injustice has declined while interest in cultural injustice has risen.

The ideological positivity of multiculturalism draws attention away from the fundamental economic changes we discussed in previous chapters. In demanding that cultural groups tolerate and respect each other, multiculturalism ignores the deep and ubiquitous structural antagonisms that are now very much part of the way we live. How can cultural groups tolerate each other when they are compelled to struggle every day with the snakes-and-ladders logic of ceaseless economic competition? It is almost inevitable that as the economic fortunes of one group improve, those of another decline. How can cultural groups be brought together peaceably when in our economic lives the whole population has already descended into a Darwinian struggle for survival and supremacy? Should the traditional working class look on with openness and acceptance as other cultural groups challenge their economic interests and prompt their downward economic mobility and social humiliation?

For us, a new upsurge of multiethnic communities would be a positive development, but they cannot simply be agglomerations of competitive individuals and distinct micro communities keen to advance their own interests. If they are to be real, affective communities, they must enter the political field to overcome the structural antagonisms of the economic sphere to develop a new account of shared interests, practices and goals. These new multiethnic communities must share a coherent political belief system that bonds individuals together. Shared interests and mutual concerns grounded in political and socioeconomic reality render cultural particularities relatively trivial. The sexual orientation or religious commitments of our neighbour become unimportant if we are both fully dedicated to a shared political project that can have real economic consequences. The skin colour of a colleague becomes insignificant if they join us in a fight to end our shared suffering. Positive, really-existing multiethnic communities should not hoist cultural particularities on high, and worship them as an indicator of our vitality and progress. Rather, they should render difference insignificant by actively producing new commitments that are shared by all.

For example, if a white EDL supporter and a recently arrived Muslim immigrant were to enter into an overriding politics that unites them in a shared struggle, if the differences between them begin to appear trivial in comparison to those things they share and have in common, the animosity that stems from their distinct cultural identities would then become far less important. This is how racism is reduced – not by respecting difference and keeping distinct cultural groups apart in brittle federations, but by producing new and powerful shared concerns and projects that make the cultural particularities of one's neighbour relatively unimportant.

This process of creating new forms of togetherness banishes fear and distrust. In time, the things that bond us together supplant the things that have kept us apart, and we can take genuine rather than feigned pleasure in our shared cultural life. A shared culture grounded in political achievement and economic security provides meaning and lends colour to our lives, it exposes our ideal of togetherness to the vital reality test, and it establishes new forms of psychical security and comfort.

We can see examples of ideal multiethnic communities in many contemporary disaster films. After the seas have risen, after a huge asteroid has struck the earth and after millions have died – and as the survivors begin to rebuild some semblance of civilisation – the cultural particularities that once preoccupied us can be seen from the communal parallax view that liberal culture ideologically disavows. Skin colour is rendered quite trivial. People are compelled to seek mutual support. Our surface differences are now unimportant. The things we have in common have taken precedence.

There is a multitude of less dramatic examples. During the industrial era, the immediacy of personal experience and a shared relationship with the means of production tended to mean that racism at work was much less apparent than we might tend to assume. We can see a vestige of this in settings such as NHS canteens, where people from many different cultural backgrounds find mutual respect as they work together with a distinct purpose. In time, the strange peculiarities of the other become less threatening, and then they become mundane. We begin to see similarity where before we were sure that no similarity existed. We see that the other strives towards a goal roughly equivalent to our own. We see that they too are subject to the external forces that shape our lives and begin to understand them more clearly. But all of this happens only when we become capable of identifying common interests. This is not simply about familiarity. New positive and comprehensible commonalities must be discovered to replace culture's fascistic mysteries. The things we have in common must eventually supersede those things that hitherto have keep us apart.

This image of a really-existing multiethnic community is directly antagonistic to the multiculturalism advocated by the liberal left today. The broad post-socialist (and often anti-socialist) liberal left hope only to arrange a truce between the various micro communities of the insecure and competitive contemporary capitalist post-social milieu (see Winlow and Hall, 2013). They hope to shame racists into abandoning their bigotry. They hope to encourage each group to tolerate the various particularities and perceived advantages of other groups. They encourage everyone to be a little bit nicer to each other: more tolerant, more forgiving, more sympathetic. There are good intentions here, and we do not wish to dismiss this project altogether, but we can now see that it is hopelessly premature because, quite clearly, liberal multiculturalists have little interest in creating the stable socioeconomic conditions and shared politics in which a new cultural conviviality might flourish. Rather, we are all told to tolerate those who compete against us for scarce resources. We are all told to respect those who appear to show no respect for our own economic interests. Inevitably, the truce breaks down and the myth of multiculturalism is revealed. Deep animosity, fear and competition are not addressed or overcome. They are simply monitored by a supposedly benevolent neoliberal state that tries as much as it can to see that everyone toes the line and abides by the rules of capitalism's interminable competition.

It is now time for critical social scientists to investigate western multiculturalism with renewed vigour. No doubt Western Europe's experiment with multiculturalism began with the best of intentions. However, we must now wrestle with the suggestion that it has actively assisted in the production of its own opposite. Populist nationalist movements are on the march across Europe, and have already achieved significant success. Ethnic tensions appear to be rising rather than receding, and it makes no sense to dismiss all who oppose mass immigration and the rapid mixing of cultures, ethnicities and religions as a minority of fascists and racists at the margins who can be safely ignored. Almost four million people voted for UKIP in the 2015 general election. In France, Marine Le Pen's National Front have made huge strides, and have clearly achieved enough popularity to disrupt the domination of the Republican and Socialist parties in the years ahead. We need to think again about how civil society can overcome anxiety and hostility, but, from the outset, it is vital that we recognise that no progress will be made unless there is concerted political action to address the structural injustices and unforgiving economic competition that lie underneath rising ethnic tensions.

We must also be honest enough to acknowledge the importance of identifying an enemy. We should dismiss the standard liberal assumption that true progress comes only through a dispassionate negotiation in which each party is willing to concede something to their opponent. Identifying an enemy creates the dialectical tension that can push history forwards. But who should be identified as our enemy? Certainly not Muslims, or any other ethnic or religious minority. We should now have no qualms whatsoever in identifying the plutocratic global business class as our principal enemy, the blockage that renders free-flowing progress impossible. Occupy usefully identified this group as the 1%, the oppressive minority that has seized control of the global financial system and corrupted democratic politics to ensure that its interests are left unchallenged. At this point in our history, and given the titanic problems that lie before us, we simply cannot allow ourselves to tolerate their obscene greed and immoral self-interest any longer. This is a fight we must win. We cannot negotiate, because no middle path exists that can lead us away from the problems we face now and those that await us in the near future.

The war on metropolitan liberals and the failure of the EDL

We discovered that many working-class white people are anxious about growing numbers of Muslims in England, but for the most part, these people were unwilling to attend an EDL protest. The reasons for this were in most cases perfectly straightforward: they didn't want to get involved in violence, and they feared they might get arrested. They feared that if they were identified as supporters of the EDL they could lose their jobs. In some cases they were simply apathetic and unwilling to actually give up their own time to publically support the movement. Many were pleased that the EDL existed and agreed with its anti-Muslim discourse, but heading out on to the streets to shout and be shouted at didn't figure highly on their list of priorities. They were happy to offer their support from the sidelines. This was especially true of older men who were angry at the lack of investment and reasonably secure jobs in their areas, and worried by the arrival in England of so many immigrants, especially Muslim immigrants, in the last decade or so. They regarded protesting as a young man's game. They would have liked to go but felt they were no longer up to it. They didn't have the energy. We also encountered many working-class women who generally supported the EDL's strident hatred of immigration and Islamism. Again, they were too busy to go along on protests, or they assumed that protesting in this way was really a 'man thing', and may well involve violence and arrest.

What all these supporters wanted was for the EDL to take the next step on their behalf. They wanted the EDL to move away from street protests towards securing its status as a legitimate political party. They would have been happy voting for the EDL, especially if support grew and there appeared to be a real chance of winning office. Voting, of course, requires only minimal time and commitment. These people were busy with other things and, generally, they were uninterested in politics. If the chance came their way to register their dissatisfaction with the number of Muslims coming into the country, they would take it. Other than that, they didn't really want to get involved.

However, the EDL supporters cannot take seriously a mainstream political spectacle in which the same political groups that have been emphasising the benefits of multiculturalism now seek to make gestures about curbing immigration as an insurance premium on a possible change of public mood. Our contacts are not wrong about the liberal middle-class's hypocrisy and ineptitude, but they have associated their intuition with the wrong reasons, a fatal mistake that has contributed to their inevitable slide into failure.

Some of those we spoke to hated the vaguely composed left-leaning 'liberal class' with such a passion that we should briefly pause to consider whether the politics of the EDL might incorporate in some way an elementary unconscious drive to self-sabotage its own project. Clearly, many supporters of the EDL are desperate to wrestle free from the liberal elite's catastrophic guidance. However, this powerful urge to totally discard those they believe to be 'useless lefties', and by extension, any suggestion of left-leaning forms of political intervention, also means they abandon a range of values, ideals, strategies and historical lessons that could, if attention were to be refocused on serious intervention in political economy, be central to the only type of politics capable of advancing their own interests. Furthermore, it is clear that the absence of an educated vanguard has limited the EDL to occasional street protests. The EDL has been unable to take the next step, despite the fact that anti-immigrant sentiments drift, with every passing day, closer and closer to the political mainstream.

This is where UKIP came in. Many who supported the EDL but were unwilling to attend an EDL street protest made it clear that they would vote UKIP in coming elections because it was a party dedicated to putting an end to immigration. Few had any idea of UKIP's broader policy agenda. Little knowledge was shown of its commitment to the neoliberal economic model or its desire to shrink the welfare state. In every case what mattered was its commitment to ending immigration. Many believed that UKIP was simply a more formal and more acceptable version of the EDL. The two groups were virtually synonymous, and it was this fact that seemed to sound the death-knell for the EDL. The rough-hewn street politics of the EDL would be overtaken by the polished, media-savvy and increasingly influential UKIP.

As UKIP gained ground, the EDL's hatred of Muslims and immigration no longer appeared particularly radical. Fear and hatred of immigrants was moving towards the mainstream. People no longer had to go through the discomforts of protest to register their desire to see immigration curtailed. They could simply vote for UKIP, which required much less effort. If UKIP achieved success, there was a chance that something might actually be done to end immigration. The EDL remained as an enervated and sporadic street movement. It may once have possessed grander ambitions, but the absence of an informed leadership capable of securing the commitment of the vast majority of supporters confined it to the street. It couldn't formalise its project, and it had no real plan to impact national or regional policy-making.

Inevitably, as our study progressed, the numbers turning up to protests began to decline. People once committed to the movement began to fall away. Many reached the firm conclusion that the movement could go no further. It was the same story over and over again. They would turn up in a town or city, they would be surrounded by police, they would do a bit of shouting, and then they would be back on the bus heading home with a feeling of having accomplished very little. Nothing changed.

Gradually, over the course of our project, those we spoke to who were involved with the EDL appeared to form the view that the group was ultimately quite impotent and incapable of effecting the kinds of change that suggested victory.

Many of our contacts who were active in street protests were or had been involved in football hooliganism. Heading to a street protest in another town or city was just like going to an away game, and for a time, that's what they liked about it. They would start drinking early on, maybe have a few lines of cocaine and a bit of a laugh with the lads, then they would experience the adrenaline of spilling off the coach to be surrounded by opponents, and quite often the police. There was also a chance they might get to throw a few punches, and return home with a story to tell. Thus the excitement of the moment was a key part of the attraction of street protesting, but as time passed, the huge numbers of police officers present at protests took a lot of the fun out of it. The sense of excitement ebbed away. It was fun to be in on something right from the beginning. There was a sense of hope and ambition that came from being surrounded by so many of one's peers. But as time passed, it became harder and harder to retain this. The hard-liners kept turning up, but the majority of others began to drift away.

The EDL didn't have an identifiable political project, but had they possessed an intellectual vanguard, things could have been quite different. Some thought Tommy Robinson had done quite a good job heading up the movement. Others thought he was a grass, or that he'd been bought off and was only in it for the money. Most were happy that the EDL didn't have a clear leadership, but the absence of a true leader capable of inspiring men and women quite clearly contributed to the movement's gradual disintegration. A true leader could have given the movement a clearer purpose and identified means of achieving clear goals. A true leader could have drawn others to the movement and dragged the group away from aimless street protests, and set them to the task of actually beginning to impact on the policies of the traditional parties of Westminster. A true leader could have attracted money and influence before beginning the process of actually taking power. A true leader could have inspired pissed-off men and women from across the country and drawn them towards a project of working-class nationalism. But those involved in the movement didn't want a leader. It was intrinsically and inexorably anarchistic. They wanted to do it their way. They didn't want their movement to be usurped and dragged off course. They didn't want to weaken their approach or capitulate to the metropolitan elite. They wanted to show everyone that they would not back down, and their desire to restrict themselves to this brief symbolic show of discontent and neglect a long-term political strategy may have contributed to their unconscious commitment to their own inevitable failure. Quite probably, we often thought, the EDL did not really want to exist in any positive political sense.

The EDL couldn't find a leader or a political ideology because it was a reluctant and fragile entity forged purely on postmodern cynicism and negativity. This begs an important question. What would have happened had some updated variant of the traditional left still existed with enough electoral power to usurp the liberal class's dominance, and actually transform economic insecurity and competitive individualism into a more stable platform that made just and convivial social relations possible? At this point we should remind ourselves that some elements of the traditional left had once sought to move beyond capitalism. The traditional left was built on a firm commitment to equality, security and common ownership. Its politics were structured in relation to a progressive account of solidarity and togetherness. In the left's traditional discourse, workers of all genders and from all ethnic backgrounds were encouraged to believe that their problems were caused by the same historical force. The traditional left believed that the profit motive and the rampant profit-seeking of the business class encouraged self-interest, broke apart communities, and caused innumerable harms throughout the social order. They worked hard to convince ordinary men and women that this account of social disruption and harm was true, and that capitalism itself was their ultimate enemy.

If we put to one side their fetishised Islamophobia, it is not too difficult to imagine these men and women being quite taken by the left's traditional account of class struggle, in the heat and light of which this irrational hatred of a misrecognised enemy could not survive. However, they knew of no leftist political project dedicated to advancing the interests of the working class. The industrial working class should have been absolutely integral to the development of leftist politics in England. Some of its most noted proponents had worked in industry and proudly carried with them the cultural characteristics of the industrial working class. But, as we saw in the previous chapter, their influence had been usurped and marginalised by the liberal middle class. But none of this mattered to our contacts. They had no knowledge of their own history. The left they despised was the left of today, a left now totally dominated by a university-educated middle class, a left dominated by identity politics, a left totally devoid of authentic working-class representatives. Our contacts simply couldn't picture a left that was dedicated to improving the economic prospects of the working class.

Our contacts hated this liberal class with a passion, and they believed that the entirety of the political left was made up of such people. There was absolutely nothing in the liberal left's discourse that appealed to them. Their hatred was such that they tended to actively position themselves by default in opposition to every idea or policy suggestion that appeared to emerge from this source. The liberal left had disappeared through the looking glass into some weird hippy dream world in which people got along without any problems. The liberal left refused to acknowledge the cloud of conflict, enmity and fear that enshrouded the decaying post-industrial towns and cities of England. Each problem our contacts raised was dismissed by the liberal left as overblown and unimportant, or a simple by-product of their racism, or their homophobia, their fear of 'otherness', or some other encultured irrational drive. The liberal left appeared to think that all we needed to do was get rid of the fascists, protect the NHS and chase down some more tax revenue, and everything would be fine. "They've got no idea. They don't know what the world is really like. They don't know how bad things have become." Versions of this dour interpretation of post-political Britain were repeated to us over and over again.

Despite the EDL supporters' justifiable anger and their attempt to escape the middle-class's misleading tutelage and corrupt politics, the political project they have created is not the project England's working class need at this point in its history. Muslims are not the enemy of the white working class, or the cause of their problems. It was not the arrival of large numbers of Muslim migrants that condemned the white working class to economic redundancy. Muslims may signify a form of cultural change greatly feared by the white working class, but the truth is that it is not the increased proximity of Muslims that has transformed the community life of the white working class.

Beyond the foreground of ethnic hatred lie the noble aims of securing a degree of economic justice and reconstituting functional community life throughout the country. However, if our contacts are to achieve these goals, they must identify capitalism itself as the fundamental force that fractured their communities and destabilised their employment. It is capitalism itself – and its central principle of unequal exchange – that drives competition, hatred and conflict. The untrammelled supremacy of liberal capitalism has pumped a fog of desperation, fear and anxiety throughout the lifeworlds of an effectively depoliticised white working class that can see no way out of its current difficulties. We all need to think clearly about what the continued supremacy of liberal capitalism will mean for civil society. Our contacts need a leftist discourse that advocates economic security, collectivism, community protection, equality and solidarity, and it needs to broadcast these principles throughout the education system, and make some attempt to do the same via mass media. They need a left that promises to work towards a utopia in which every man, woman and child is valued equally. They need a left that creates and is then led by intelligent and articulate members of the working class. They need a left that promises to defend the interests of the working class come hell or high water, a left that will not run away at the first sign of trouble, and a left that believes totally in both the virtue and feasibility of its aims. In England today, no such left exists. Once again, from the ashes of defeat, it must be recreated.

SIX

The scapegoat

It is only recently, with the election of Jeremy Corbyn as leader of the Labour Party, that we have seen the regulation of the market returning to a position of prominence in mainstream leftist economic policy in Britain. We will see, in the years to come, whether this actually comes to anything in the face of a ferocious and long-running attack by the entrenched liberal elites who wield such power in the Labour Party and the mainstream media. The Blairites still might engineer a comeback. The scale of capitalism's victory is particularly striking when we remember key Blairite figures utilising right-wing rhetoric about the fundamental benefits of free market capitalism. Here is Peter Mandelson, at the time Secretary of State for Trade and Industry in Blair's first Labour government, on the approach to aphoristic eloquence: 'We want a society that celebrates and values its business heroes as much as its pop stars and footballers. So we must remove the barriers to enterprise in this country, reward risk-taking, and encourage innovation and creativity.'

Britain's hollowed-out electoral democracy is, quite simply, not providing ordinary men and women with an appealing vision of a better future. Only a tiny number of mainstream politicians actively endorse genuine change. The majority hope only to manage the market economy a little better, and perhaps iron out a few bureaucratic impediments here and there. The dominance of neoliberalism across a truncated political spectrum means that, when it comes to personal failure, frustration and anxiety, accounts of inadequate talent and poor decision-making tend to predominate. People believe in personal agency, hard work and meritocracy. Forty years of neoliberalism have seen to that.

If you are talented and work hard, you will rise. Alternatively, if you happen to find yourself unemployed, flat broke and alone, you have no one to blame but yourself. You have failed to take advantage of the opportunities that were provided for you. You have shown inadequate talent and fortitude. You deserve nothing better. You do not even deserve sympathy, because your personal failures mean that those who work harder have unfairly become responsible for your upkeep.

But neoliberalism's ideological centre cannot hold forever. The cynicism and pessimism that abounds in our political culture certainly does not rule out a return to politics at some point in the future. A great many people have already come to the conclusion that, without a determined corrective intervention, they will be unable to achieve the stability and security they crave. There already exists a general sense that a growing proportion of the people have grown tired of the false freedoms of the liberal epoch and again want to believe. They want something to happen. They want their frustrations to be taken seriously. They await an appealing political narrative that identifies the cause of their troubles and promises to fix things.

When progressive political narratives about challenging entrenched economic power and advancing the interests of the working class are in a weakened state and no longer appear to have much to offer, alternative political traditions begin to garner support. Communities rummage around in search of something that can be presented as the objective cause of their frustration and anxiety. The community needs someone or something to blame for its parlous circumstances. It hopes to restore tranquillity to its emotional life by justly punishing those who have been identified as the cause of their individual and collective suffering. In such an environment it becomes increasingly likely that the community, in its desperation, will identify an ethnic or religious minority that can be pathologised and blamed. We have already seen that in the absence of an explanation rooted in political economy the EDL have identified Muslims as the objective cause of their frustration and anxiety. But precisely what is it about Muslim community life that inspires such anger and opprobrium among supporters of the EDL?

The gods of fortune must be assuaged...

We start with Kenny. He is 45. He is not a particularly dedicated follower of the EDL, but his account of the problems caused by Muslims fits together perfectly with other EDL supporters we have spoken to. Kenny makes most of his money trading in the illicit economy. He aspires to a much higher standard of living, but he is greatly frustrated by what he sees as the untrammelled economic competitiveness of the local Muslim community. He has this to say:

> 'Where I live, they [Muslims] are the ones with the nice cars, the big houses, their kids running round like jack the lads in Mercs and Beemers [Mercedes and BMW cars] that have been bought by ripping us off in their shops for a pint of milk while they look after their own.'

Like many others, Kenny's general hatred of Muslims is understood in relation to a range of local issues and personal experiences. In spoken accounts, these local issues are positioned as indicative of the fundamental problems that lie at the core of Islam, and they are used to evidence his claim that the white working class are downward mobile, and ignored by political elites. Kenny also uses snippets of personal experience to drive home his message about the injustices of the present. Being poorly treated by an Asian shopkeeper is immediately understood as an indication of the hatred Muslims feel toward the white working class. Being disrespected by affluent Muslims keen to display their consumer success reflects the obscene self-interest that lies at the core of their community.

Kenny sees Muslims as ferocious economic competitors who have risen through the social hierarchy at great speed. They have done this by corrupting the system wherever possible, assisting fellow Muslims at every opportunity, and systematically cheating and undermining the neighbouring white working class who continue to play by the rules. Kenny is particularly frustrated that recently arrived immigrants are able to consume at a level well beyond that which his own meagre circumstances allow. He is sure that he works hard, contributes and deserves much better.

Young Mike offers a similar interpretation:

> 'What I can't understand is the money thing. Where does the money come from to buy up all the shops? They've got all the pizza places, all the Indians, all the burgers places, newsagents, off license, everything. Where does that come from? I thought they were supposed to be skint, starving to death, and that's why we let them in? And then they can't speak the language but they can afford to drive around in brand new top of the range motors? [...] There's loads of [white working–class] lads who can't get a house to live in, right? Loads. Loads moving into bedsits, loads back with their Mams. Who gets the decent houses? Who? Muslims. Exactly... it doesn't matter that other people who were born here have been waiting for a [council] house for years and years. This is why people get angry. It's just the unfairness of it.'

Big Waz:

> 'It's money. It's jobs. This is what gets people pissed off. They can't see the fairness of it. They work all their lives and they've got fuck all, but you see straight off the boat immigrants driving around in flash motors, pocket full of cash, right? Shops all over the place, buying up houses. They [that is, those who support the EDL] think, what's happening here? This isn't right.'

David also focuses first on local issues that affect him and what remains of his community. Recent grooming cases are at the forefront of his mind:

> 'You see them in flash cars and all that. Where the fuck do they get the money for that? And did you see on the box [the TV] about them grooming cases?...

156

Gangs of Pakis picking up young white lasses and locking them up… How many cases have there been? How many young kiddies are we talking about? It's not a small problem; it's everywhere. Everywhere it's going on. Bradford, Rotherham, Rochdale, Birmingham, all over the place. And what we've heard about is just the start. More will come out, it's bound to.

'Wherever you've got a big group of Muslims living you've got grooming. I can't understand it, because this should be front page news. It should be, like, the main thing the politicians have to deal with. The police should be all over it, but there's just nothing. It gets ignored, people keep quiet about it… It makes me feel fucking sick. They want fucking hanging for that, and people's too scared to talk about it coz you get called a racist. People around here are fucking done with it.

'What gets me, right, [about grooming cases] is that it's been proved the police knew about them cases. They knew that these dirty bastards had taken these young kids, right? They knew. And they did nothing. Why? Because they knew if they did something about it they'd get called racists. See, this is what they've [the liberal left] done, this is what political correctness has done. It's madness. People are shit scared of talking about these fuckers because they don't want to be badged as a racist. They've stopped caring about the kids. These are little kids we're talking about. The kids don't matter according to them. Honestly, how can you not get angry when you hear about this? How can you not think, something needs to do done about these fucking Muslims?'

The sexual abuse of vulnerable white girls by gangs of Asian men prompted a lot of angry discussion. Just as our research was beginning to get off the ground, a number of grooming cases came to light, and for a time these cases were all our contacts talked about. As we will see, they would begin to attribute other problematic behaviours and beliefs to Muslims, but then the focus would return to abuse and paedophilia. The collective anger of our contacts was, quite clearly, not simply a product of an instrumental drive to defend and advance their economic interests. Here is David again:

> 'You've got to remember a lot of them is just coming over for the money. They can sign on, get a house, all the benefits. I saw on the box [the TV] that loads of them are just sending the cash straight back home. Not looking for work or anything. That's just fucking robbery that is. Why the fuck should I be paying money [in tax] and it ends up paying for someone over in Pakistan or Romania or wherever the fuck it is?'

Brad is 38. He has a good job, and he is certainly more affluent than many of his peers quoted in these pages. His stake in the mainstream economy has, however, not encouraged him to attenuate his critique of England's Muslim community. He picks up on a point raised earlier by David:

> 'I'll tell you what's mental mate, what's absolutely mental: You know that there's evidence that loads of them, thousands right, they're just claiming the benefits and sending it straight back over to Pakistan, Afghanistan, all them places? Even them that's working, all the money goes straight back out of the country. This is why our economy's on its arse. Money is just flying out of the country. Whole areas out there are being rebuilt off the money what's sent back. Look, they don't pay tax. None of them. I see it all the time. They don't care. It's just the money. They're here for the money. It's mad... [they are] scamming the social [security system], getting all the housing benefit, all the dole money, not doing anything and sending it all back.'

Again, grooming cases become the focus of discussion. Many of our respondents seemed sure that the best way to convince our researcher of the pathologies of the Islamic faith was to focus on the involvement of Muslim men in organised paedophilia. Brad continues:

> 'It's when you hear about the grooming cases you really see how bad things have gone. I mean, for fuck's sake: you've got these young girls, dead young, right, and they're being pimped out by these dirty fucking Paki fuckers. Gangs of them are abusing these girls. And do you know why? It's because they've been taught that white girls are there for the taking. White girls have no morals, no decency. You can fuck a white girl and it doesn't matter, but you can't fuck a Paki girl because that's shameful, the family won't like it. No sex before marriage and all that. But white girls, they're different. Do what you like. And these are young kids, right, not even teenagers. They should still be playing with dolls but they're in the back of some dirty Paki's taxi being gang-raped by a bunch of fucking Muslim scum.

> 'When I think about it I think about my niece and nephew. What if it was them that got picked up by these cunts? That's what I think of. Some of the stories, some of the court cases, well, it's just fucking horrible, isn't it? Just horrible. And to be honest, you won't like this, you'll probably think I'm a cunt, but to be honest, they want killing for that. No mercy. All paedophiles, mate, all of them. I'd have no mercy. You get caught once and that's it, you're gone.'

Paul joins in:

> 'What kind of world are we living in when this kind of thing goes on, eh? And you're not even allowed to say that it's a bunch of Muslim's what's done it. You can't say it because it's racist. But look what they've

done. They've driven around and they've picked up that girl because she's white. They treated her worse than shit because she's white. And we're racist?

'To be honest, there are so many people around here pissed off about it that you could honestly see something major happening. People don't like to discuss it because it's, well, it's too hard to take. People don't want to talk about it, do they? But I'll tell you one thing, it's making more and more people come out against Muslims, against immigration. People won't go on a protest because they think there's going to be trouble. They think they're going to get arrested. They scared, right? Fair enough. But anymore of these cases and you'll see things change.'

Big Baz was one of our most vocal contacts. He appeared absolutely sure that the problems faced by the white working class stemmed from the growing numbers and entrenchment of Muslims of England. Here he provides a quick recap of the issues:

'See, you've got to put everything together. You've got your grooming cases, right? Then you've got suicide bombers in London. You've got these preachers saying everyone should fight jihad, right? You've got killings in France, Spain, everywhere. You've got terrorism everyday now. You see terrorists getting arrest on the news all the time. You've got Lee Rigby getting cut up in the middle of the street, broad daylight. Then you've got Asian gangs, drugs, you've got places where white people can't go, haven't you? It's just daft that nothing's been done. Then you've got Sharia law, and 10 other things I can't think of. Now, to me, that adds up to a massive, massive threat.'

In this quote David focuses on the perceived economic competitiveness of English Muslims:

David: 'What gets on a lot of people's tits is you see them [Muslims] all the time, [and] loads of them are obviously just playing the system. The young [Muslim] lads always have flash cars, don't they? I see them outside the school, showing off. Go down the town and you'll see them walking about in gangs, and they've all got bags of new clothes, all got the best of gear on. I'm not bothered by all that to be honest, but the young ones, well, it doesn't look fair does it? To them it looks like they're taking the piss, especially when loads of them can't even speak the language. They get fucked off, and well, fair enough, really. They think, where's my new gear? Where's my new car? Part-time job is the best they can do. And then you get to thinking, where's the money come from? A lot of the businesses round here are Muslim-owned, and obviously that pisses people off. They get angry. Even shops in the town now, a lot are Muslim-owned. And then you see the money. You see them looking after their own. People think, there's no way they're paying the tax, there's no way they're not cheating somehow. Plus, now, you've got drugs, you've got gangs. You just add it all together and people get the idea what's happening. People can see that they're being fucked over. That's how the hate starts.'

Interviewer: 'Is there any jealousy in it then?'

David: 'Not really, I don't think. Not jealousy. Because people see that Muslims just don't care. They just look after their own. They don't want to pay taxes. They don't care about the schools, about the community. They couldn't care less if the place turns to shit. The things we care about they don't care about. They've not integrated, they don't want to integrate. I think a lot of the lads see it differently. Not all but some of them do care. They want a job for themselves, but they want to see places like this get stronger again...

They see how things have gone. They know the country's gone down the tubes. Lots of the older lads are worried about their kids. They see what's happening now, and they think, how's our lad going to get a job? How's he going to get on when all this is happening? So it's not jealousy, not really.'

Ripped off

Many of our contacts considered the exploitation of an apparently indulgent welfare system to be a form of theft. Behind this account often lay an uncomplicated racism. The welfare system was, in their view, 'theirs', the property of the indigenous white population. As a direct consequence of this assumption, the money claimed by immigrant groups and ethnic minorities had been stolen. The welfare state was there for the indigenous white population and no one else. However, not all of our contacts subscribed entirely to this model. Many of the men we spoke to offered quite an aggressive critique of white welfare claimants, and considered all of those reliant on welfare to be skivers living off the hard work of others, and many blamed politicians for making the welfare system a soft touch.

Many also spoke of the millions of pounds that they believed had been poured into Muslim neighbourhoods with a view to preventing the radicalisation of Muslim youth. They also spoke of Muslim-owned businesses profiting from the misfortunes of the surrounding white working class. There was not a lot by way of evidence to substantiate these claims, but this mattered little. Our contacts certainly appeared to believe that these claims were true, and these claims were then used to bolster other claims that suggested that Muslims were a malign presence within English civil society that must be taken to task and then dispensed with all together. Some focused on inward-looking Muslim communities that assisted their members to get ahead at the expense of the indigenous population. Ruthless entrepreneurialism was, apparently, being cultivated at the heart of these communities, and Muslim businessmen and women apparently took pride in cheating the system, especially of tax revenue, and cheating the local white population, especially by charging exorbitant prices in their shops.

Muslims, apparently, had their hand out for every benefit going, and they steadfastly refused to pay any tax. In this respect, our contacts tended to focus on the presence of Muslims in the local economy, and the proliferation of Muslim-owned shops that were, essentially, 'cash businesses'. Our contacts were sure Muslim businessmen and women were playing the system at least in part because they had already decided that Muslims were a negative presence that disturbed what would otherwise be a peaceful and progressive England in which the indigenous white population thrived.

Our contacts already knew that Muslims had been involved in terrorist bombings, murders and the sexual exploitation of children. Some also appeared to have detailed local knowledge of the involvement of Muslim men in markets for illegal drugs, and other forms of street crime. For them it was not too much of a stretch to imagine the involvement of Muslim men in any number of horrific social activities. If Muslims were involved in business, they must be cheating in some way. If a young Muslim man was spotted driving an expensive sports car, it must have been bought with the proceeds of crime, or cheating of some kind.

As we have already seen, the consumer successes of younger Muslim populations angered many of our contacts. Again, their frustration stemmed from their inability to consume at a roughly equivalent level. Generally, our contacts were locked into unstable, competitive and poorly paid labour markets, and some were at least partially reliant on welfare. They wanted to buy fast cars and designer clothes, but they could not. When they saw recently arrived immigrants display the trappings of success, they bristled with indignation. The successes of recently arrived immigrants reinforced the sense that they, the old proletarian class, were falling rapidly to the very bottom, and that they were quickly becoming increasingly irrelevant in a consumerised, liberalised and tech-savvy 21st-century England.

High-end consumerism, our contacts appeared to think, should be the preserve of the indigenous white population. It simply wasn't fair that those who were not born in the country were consuming at such a high level while the scattered remnants of the old white working class were forced to scratch a living together by any means possible. And here again we encounter an obvious contradiction. Everyone we spoke to appeared convinced that Muslims refused to integrate into English civil society. Many pointed to the religious dress of reasonably devote Muslims as evidence of this. However, our contacts also problematised those Muslims who appeared keen to integrate into the consumerised spectacle of English popular culture. When presented with this apparent anomaly, our contacts shifted the goalposts. When they talked about integration, they didn't mean consumerism and economic success. They were concerned mostly with values and tradition, and they could see no evidence that Muslims were willing to commit to the basic principles of the English way of life.

This 'English way of life' was also poorly sketched out. Our contacts certainly could not agree on what it was, but whatever it was, they could agree that Muslims refused to adopt its principles. The prejudice of our contacts preceded the events on which they focused. They believed that their critique of Muslims in England was rational and evidence-based. However, at a deeper level, they were committed to the view that the Muslim population was a problem for English society, and so wherever they looked, they were able to identify evidence that supported this belief.

Our contacts also complained that huge amounts of money were being spent regenerating Muslim areas. For some, this money indicated that radical Islamist terror campaigns had achieved a degree of success not often acknowledged by political or popular culture. The state, understandably keen to reduce the terrorist threat and the radicalisation of young Muslim men and women, had loosened the purse strings to make sure that Muslim areas had good quality housing, youth clubs and a variety of other services. Young Muslims, apparently, were benefiting from new job opportunities and work programmes that had been created to integrate a population judged 'at risk'. The government, apparently, was doing everything it could to boost Muslim standards of living with a view to incorporating the Muslim community into the consumerised circuits of everyday life in the west.

Some of our contacts even contended that they had encountered workplace discrimination as a result of this new governmental favouritism. Large corporations were now, apparently, keen to boost their recruitment of minorities, first, because it made the corporation look open, honest and 'multicultural', and second, because there were direct financial advantages in the form of tax deductions and government grants. Again, the veracity of these claims is not particularly important. When views such as this were vocalised in groups dominated by men who supported the EDL, the assembled throng immediately exhibited a popularised form of confirmation bias. To these men, such claims sounded true because they had already concluded that Muslims were a problem for English civil society, that Muslims were favoured by the political class, and that the white working class was now being discriminated against by an establishment dominated by those committed to multiculturalism.

White hot hatred

In this respect, the caricature of the Muslim immigrant created by the EDL is quite similar to the caricature of the Jew popularised in Germany by Nazis during the 1930s. Ultimately, the EDL's caricature of the Muslim immigrant functioned as a blank screen onto which EDL supporters could project a range of negative characteristics. Our contacts were sure that there was nothing that was positive in Muslim communities. They were sure that the presence of Muslims was corrupting English economic and cultural life. The surety of these things then enabled our contacts to attribute to Muslims a host of negative characteristics that appear to have little to do with the reality of everyday life in Muslim communities. Everything that was considered vulgar, backward, violent and pathological was, they believed, to be found in Muslim communities.

We see this particularly clearly when we investigate our contacts' accounts of the involvement of Muslim men in the sexual exploitation of vulnerable white children. We have no doubt whatsoever that our contacts were truly aggrieved by these cases. Many of those we spoke to were quite clearly disturbed by these narratives of systematised and long-running child abuse. Understandably, they wanted those involved to be punished severely. They also wanted action to be taken to ensure that such things could not happen again. However, while our contacts displayed genuine concern for the victims, their account is inevitably tied to the religious and ethnic background of the abusers. Our contacts were, of course, disgusted by all paedophilia. However, when they encountered stories of abuse involving white perpetrators, the religious and ethnic background of the perpetrator was treated as an irrelevance. For example, while we were conducting our research, the newspapers were full of stories of systematised sexual abuse that stemmed from the Jimmy Savile investigation. It had been proven that Savile, for decades a popular TV personality, had abused hundreds of children over the course of his career. Other criminal investigations were underway that focused on a number of Savile's contemporaries, and there were also suggestions that a paedophile ring, including a number of notable politicians, had operated for many years with apparent impunity at the heart of Westminster. There were also stories of sexual abuse in children's homes and other institutions. Inevitably, when our contacts gathered together, talk turned to these investigations. As one would expect, there were off-colour jokes and suchlike, but the general mood was one of utter disgust. These men hated paedophiles, and having white skin did not protect the paedophile from their hatred.

Some of our contacts believed that these cases were further evidence of the hideous corruption that lay at the heart of our media and political systems. Some had researched these cases, and they were aware of suggestions that attempts had been made to cover up systemic sexual abuse. Here is David talking about this subject:

'It's amazing when you hear the stories. I can't believe that people didn't know what was going on. When you've got abuse on that scale, loads of people are going to know about it. Now it comes out that they've covered everything up for years. People have been paid off. It's just, I can't really find the words. Who does something like that to a little kid? These weirdos are running the country don't forget. They just think they can do whatever they like, and the police, whatever, they're not going to do anything about it. The kids, their families, they don't count. They're nothing. I can't find the words. It all wants burning down, the lot of it.'

These stories bolstered our contacts' hatred of the metropolitan middle class, who they believed were running the country, but the ethnic background of the elite sex offenders exposed by the media was in every case totally ignored. The opposite is true of our contacts' analysis of sex crimes involving Muslim men. Here, the ethnic background of the offender is used to evidence the claim that all Muslims are capable of utterly repugnant crimes, and that the Islamic faith's total disregard for non-believers is the ultimate issue at stake. The apparent proliferation of grooming cases in which Muslims men were the principal offenders suggested to our contacts that something rotten and barbarous lay at the core of the Islamic faith, and these cases were simply the first horrific consequences that had made their way to the surface. Other horrors, our contacts were sure, would inevitably follow. Muslims were encouraged to believe that white women could be used and thrown away. Muslims were encouraged to believe that the white population were vulgar, promiscuous and amoral. Muslims protected their own, and everyone else was identified as an enemy to be cheated or abused with impunity. The sheer number of these cases, our contacts were sure, suggested that the sexual exploitation of vulnerable white children was, in fact, common practice. If 10 cases had come to light, the reality was probably that 50 or 100 Muslim paedophile rings were in operation. This was not simply a case of a few bad apples. Rather, the entire barrel was spoiled and rotten. The entire Muslim community carried with them a hatred for the indigenous white population.

When our contacts encountered Muslims who appeared friendly and open, they took this as evidence of their conniving nature. Muslims, it was argued, were often friendly on the surface to get the local white population off guard. Ultimately, they hated England, the white race and anyone who was not also Muslim. Muslims were utterly dedicated to advancing their collective interests at the expense of every other social group. Beneath the surface they were disgusted by the permissiveness of Western culture and saw the local white population as dirty and ignorant. They wanted money and power, but their ultimate goal was to enforce their religion and culture on England in order to cleanse it of its barbarism.

All of this fed into the EDL's vortex of negativity that fuelled an unabashed hatred of Muslims. Of course, some of our contacts maintained that they did not hate Muslims. Rather, they believed that the Muslim faith and aspects of Muslim culture were incompatible with English society, and in such a situation, it should not be English society that had to change to accommodate Muslim belief. The majority, however, acknowledged their hatred, but believed that they were simply responding in kind to the hatred shown to them by Muslims. Who could deny that Muslims hated the indigenous white population? How much evidence did one need before it became reasonable to reach such a conclusion? Muslims were attacking western interests all over the globe. Islamic terrorist groups were dedicated to killing as many non-Muslim westerners as possible. Even apparently law-abiding and respectable English Muslims despised England's white population. Grooming cases proved this beyond all doubt. Quite clearly Muslims imagined that the white working class were godless and amoral heathens, there to be exploited.

As we've seen, our contacts quite often suggested that Muslim communities were dedicated to 'looking after their own'. For some, this was but one indication of a broader Muslim conspiracy to take over the country in order to enforce Sharia law and the Islamic faith. Others suggested that Muslim communities were pathologically inward-looking, and totally unwilling to assimilate. Muslims were always presented as inextricably bonded to culture and religion. No other aspect of personal identity was considered important. EDL supporters were sure that Muslims were always first and foremost Muslims. Our contacts appeared to believe that other aspects of Muslim identity were insignificant and not worth discussing. Religious belief and cultural commitment appeared to them to constitute the whole of Muslim identity rather than a mere part of it.

Ultimately, according to our contacts, Muslims could never assimilate into broader English culture because they wanted only to associate with other Muslims. Islam was fundamentally illiberal. Its followers were unwilling to tolerate religious diversity. Even when various Muslim faith leaders spoke of tolerance and peace, the truth was that they hated being surrounded by those committed to other faiths. They hated Jews, Christians, homosexuals and atheists. They were secretly disgusted by the reality of 21st-century England, and, paradoxically, they both abhorred and were strangely attracted to the libertinism and permissiveness of consumer culture. They were parochial and closed-minded, and they truly believed in their god and the rules set down in the Quran. Behind surface attempts to reach out to the English, and despite the attempts that were being made to find common ground, the truth was that Muslims were only interested in other Muslims. Everyone else was an enemy.

According to our contacts, Muslims did not consider themselves English. They did not support the nation's sports teams. They wanted only to enjoy the pleasures of their own restrictive cultural and religious life. As a consequence of their religious and cultural devotion, they were forever destined to remain separated from the main body of English civil society. They wanted to establish, defend and reproduce an alien culture at the heart of England, and they wanted the rest of the English population to recognise their right to do so. If the rest of the English population changed, if it adopted the Islamic faith and its customs, then they could gain admittance and journey towards the light. If it refused to change, it must accept the reality of the Islamic faith and Muslim community life, and stay well away.

Our contacts' desire to portray Muslim communities as pathologically inward-looking reveals the core contradiction at the heart of the EDL's discourse. As we have already seen, many supporters of the EDL were dedicated to the task of recreating and defending their own inward-looking community that 'looks after its own'. It is not too difficult to see how this theme works in tandem with their concern for the disintegration of white working-class neighbourhoods. The EDL's melancholic brooding over its own mythical lost community prompted it to look on enviously at the enjoyment Muslims took from their own community life. Again, the EDL's narrative involves the other's appropriation of cultural value. Muslim communities were believed to possess a cohesion and a reproductive logic that was now judged to be absent from white working-class neighbourhoods.

At root, our contacts appeared to carry with them the unconscious belief that Muslim communities possessed the spirit of solidarity and brotherhood precisely because white working-class communities did not. The spirit of solidarity and brotherhood – the loss of which, our contacts believed, had caused such sadness and melancholia – had, in fact, been stolen from the white working class by the hated other, who then proceeded to flaunt his community's solidarity in front of the white working class, who were then forced to look on enviously as its anger grew and mutated.

The reality is that supporters of the EDL dream of returning to a mythical time in which everything made sense, a time in which everything 'just seemed to work', and in which they were valued, respected and considered integral to the country's wellbeing. They imagine that the men of their class were once free to live a life founded on solidarity and security. Now they feel undervalued, downwardly mobile, anxious and alone, forced to fight for cultural significance in a remorselessly competitive world changing at lightning pace, and always for the worse. Once again, as the required systemic political explanation was fetishistically disavowed by mainstream culture, and, lacking the confidence and organic intellectual tradition to explain it to themselves, the EDL drew on residual racism to misrecognise Muslims as the proximal concrete objects that caused their loss.

SEVEN

Mourning and melancholia

Interviewer: 'So, if you had a time machine you'd go back to the seventies or the eighties, when you were a lad, eh?'

Tony: 'Look, all I'm saying is that things were better then. Yes, definitely, things were better. For people like me it was better. We had a right laugh at school, and, well, everything just seemed to work. There was jobs then. Everyone worked. People stuck together. And I think the truth of it is that most of the people were just happier, just, I don't know what you'd call it. It just worked, that's all... You're going to say it wasn't that great back then. Fair enough. Maybe it wasn't. But I just didn't see the bad things when I was young, and I don't think other people did either. It was, the mood of the place, it was just different. Now, everyone knows how bad things have gotten. Everyone is just, well, it's just not the same. You don't see the good things, and I used to take all that for granted... I think jobs, real jobs, is important. I think when work started to go the pride started to go. I don't know. But that's what a lot of the lads want, not really for them but for their kids. People know that things are getting worse. Everything is fucked. They want that kind of life they had when they were kids. A sense of community, isn't it? Pride in your neighbourhood. People looking out for each other and having a laugh. That's what I'm talking about.'

Interviewer: 'So why the EDL then? Why Muslims?'

Tony: 'Well, it's jobs isn't it? Jobs and a lot of other things. We lost jobs with immigration. It's obvious. And then it's people moving in, people moving out. People who couldn't give a shit about the place, couldn't care about the people, the history. It's more and more shit everywhere, everything getting worse, getting harder. It's just, we've been forgotten. We've been fucked over and no one cares. That's it, as far as I can see. Who cares now? We used to have respect and now we're all over the place... To be honest, the EDL is all done, mate. It's finished now. At least around here it is. The police, court appearances, no one can be arsed. Nothing happened really. People couldn't see the point anymore, and then, when that happens, everything just becomes a massive fuck on, you know what I mean? But it's obvious that it will come back somehow. It might not be the EDL, but it'll be something else. People will vote UKIP next time around. People want to cut immigration. People will vote for anyone who says they're going to go back to the way things were, I think. It's just common sense really. See, it was never just the EDL. People are pissed off, anyone can see that. Nothing's being done. It's like, it's just another world isn't it? I don't know... Personally I don't think UKIP will do anything. I don't trust them. But people are bound to give them a shot, because, well, what else is there?'

In this chapter we want to offer a more detailed analysis of the fundamental forces that drive the EDL. We want to strip away the ethnic hatred that lies at the forefront of the movement and ask, what is it that supporters of the EDL really want? What, ultimately, do they hope to achieve? What do they believe would happen if they were granted their heart's desire, and all Muslims and recently arrived immigrants magically disappeared from England's grey and despoiled land?

We should start by reiterating that it is now very difficult for members of the traditional working class to access reasonably remunerated forms of employment. Traditional forms of work have disappeared, and new forms of work are insecure and poorly paid (see Southwood, 2011; Lloyd, 2013; Dorling, 2015). The inability of growing numbers of people to access the consumerised mainstream foments the anger and hostility that exists in such abundance in marginalised neighbourhoods. As we have seen, people start to look around for someone or something to blame, and as we have repeatedly stressed, it is the inability – or the unwillingness – of the political left to direct the working class's attention to capitalism's market system, and the inevitable harms and injustices it produces, that ensures working people look elsewhere in order to locate a corrupting force that is destabilising their lives and degrading their experience.

Economic insecurity – and the perennial sense that one is undervalued, underpaid and locked outside what looks like a world mainlining on boundless pleasure and indulgence – is important, but it is not the only form of insecurity that shapes the discourse of the EDL. Many of our contacts appeared to carry with them an imprecise sense of foreboding and discomfort, an out-of-place-ness, that, in their naive political activity, they hoped to rectify. This sense of foreboding is closely connected to the perennial economic insecurity experienced by our contacts. As we've seen, all appeared sure that things would continue to get a lot harder for the white working class. But these were not the only issues at stake.

Some spoke in detail about a sense of sadness and frustration that stemmed from the gradual disappearance of traditional working-class community life. These traditional communities, it seems, once anchored the social experience of the old proletarian class. They provided their members with a sense of place, a sense of belief and a structure of feeling that enabled forms of psychic security to be established and reproduced across generations. Individuals were encouraged to feel at home within the borders of the community, and to take pleasure and satisfaction in its customs, traditions and pastimes (see Winlow et al, 2015, for a more detailed analysis). Once we clear away the racism and the anger, what we find at the core of the EDL is an enduring desire to return home, and to find again the security that home represents. However, they cannot return home because this home no longer exists.

Homeless

Many of our contacts found themselves in jobs they despised. There was nothing of value in these jobs for them to cling on to. They felt reduced by them, demeaned. They wanted to produce something, they wanted to work with their hands, and they wanted others to recognise the value of their labour. Instead they worked as pizza delivery drivers, removal men, security guards and shop workers. Others had managed to retain some attachment to the manual trades. We spoke to electricians, gas fitters, builders, glaziers, brick layers, mechanics, plasterers, tyre fitters, roofers and plumbers. These men tended to be a little more enthusiastic about their jobs, but the story they had to tell was not a positive one. Wages were down and insecurity and competition were up. The older men in particular were sure that today less respect is shown for craft, skill and experience. Once upon a time the ability to do a job well was highly prized. Now all that seemed to matter was how quickly and how cheaply the job could be done. Over and over again we listened to slightly different accounts of this same story. Our contacts were able to identify a process of gradual decline, and perhaps because of this they tended to assume that things were once, back in their collective history, almost perfect.

Ultimately, supporters of the EDL wanted to (re)create this mythical perfect world, this world in which they felt immediately at home and in which everything made sense. A perfect world that was given its character by a really existing community life that structured everyday experience. It was a world in which their skills were valued and their jobs paid enough money for them to live a good life free from perennial anxiety and competition. In this perfect world men like them were listened to. They had committed political representatives dedicated to the nation's security and wellbeing. It was clear to all that the old traditions were considered valuable and important, and that every member of the community was committed to their preservation. No dangerous pollutants were allowed to enter this restricted cultural space. Suspicion of outsiders was considered to be a mark of good sense. In this community, everyone knew his place, and nobody was left out. If supporters of the EDL could (re)create this mythical world, insubstantial liberalism would be dispensed with, and order, belief and security would return.

It is not simply that there is no return to this lost world of solidarity, security and belief. The sad fact is that it never existed. At least not in the way these men imagine. Even during the heyday of England's industrial working class there was considerable anxiety about external threats to the composition and reproduction of working–class community life. Traditions and cultures were believed to be constantly under attack. Something valuable was slipping away. Forces external to the community hoped to attack it and steal its substance, or to breach the barrier of the community and pollute it from the inside (see, for example, Hoggart, 1969). During the 1940s and 1950s, for example, it was common to argue that consumerism was seducing the young, and that new forms of media were transforming their values and aspirations. The old ways were being lost, and the culture looked set to slip into oblivion. Throughout modernity these arguments have persistently been heard. Indeed, all communities are subject to this sense of gradual disintegration. It is the very experience of losing a traditional culture that brings it into being.

How should we understand the desire of EDL supporters to dispense with the fakery of postmodern experience so that they might (re)create a world of security, solidarity and belief? Here it is useful to draw on Sigmund Freud's (2001) analysis of mourning and melancholia. It is common to believe that these two phrases reference the same emotions and forms of social experience. However, Freud claims that they are quite different. He suggests that mourning involves accepting and rationally coming to terms with the loss of a loved one. We accept that our beloved is gone and will not return. We are hurt by this loss. The absence of the love object affects us greatly. However, we accept that nothing can be done to return our beloved to us, and we begin slowly to move on.

Melancholy is quite different. Freud claims that melancholy results from an inability to truly accept the loss of our loved one. The melancholic remains pathologically attached to the departed. He cannot let his beloved go, and the absence of his beloved overshadows his social experience. His life is deprived of its vitality and pleasure because his beloved remains beyond his reach and unable to join him as he continues on life's journey. For the melancholic, time does not heal. Rather than fade into nothingness, the pain of separation changes and evolves. Even when, as time passes, he can speak of accepting his loss, in reality he remains tightly bonded to the departed object, and the material absence of his beloved cloaks his life in an unyielding sadness. Only the active and rehabilitative work of mourning can relieve him of his suffering.

As we have already claimed, supporters of the EDL display a fetishistic attachment to the lost historical object of traditional English proletarian culture. They refuse to accept the loss of their traditional way of life. Their decaying communities and dilapidated neighbourhoods are enshrouded in melancholy. They know that this lost world cannot be brought back into existence. However, this knowledge is for the moment too disturbing to be accepted consciously. They know that the flows of global trade cannot be reversed to re-energise England's productivist labour markets, yet they argue that our politicians must dedicate themselves to precisely this task. They know that their communities have already disappeared, and yet they argue that their communities must be defended from external forces that threaten their continuity. They know but do not want to know the truth, and so this knowledge remains trapped in the unconscious.

The politics of the EDL possesses an obviously melancholic aspect. There are occasional bouts of drunkenness and raucous carnival, but these things never communicate a sense of positivity and joy. The anger these men carry with them springs from sadness and fear. They seek to defend something that never existed in the perfect form they imagine but nevertheless had more substance than Anderson's (1983) socially constructed 'imagined community'. It was always a fragile, rickety project under permanent maintenance and reconstruction, but the partial substance of security provided by permanent employment and the hope provided by political visions of a better world still structure the memory and oral tradition. Above all it was the hope they remember, and they cling on to the hope that a new era of industrialism will dawn, new jobs will be created, and the popular perception of their class will be transformed. This wasn't Benjamin's (1996) fake hope given to wretched souls to soothe them into acquiescence, but a substantive hope, a real hope that drew its sustenance from the collective experience of incrementally improving lives on a bedrock of economic security which, by the 1960s, had a palpable existence. The kernel of the lost object is the memory of this vital type of hope – if the object is lost forever, they lose all substantive sense of hope.

They cannot bear the humiliating prospect that it will be their generation that allows the lost object of the traditional community to disappear forever. Previous generations had defended this community against powerful threats. They didn't want this community to wither and die on their watch. Consciously, they hope to continue on with the fight to defend it, even though, unconsciously, they know that this fight has already been lost. They sense that their social identities and their hope for a better future would immediately disintegrate if they were to reach the rational conclusion that the lost object of community was gone forever and could never be recovered. The pain of acceptance would be too great, so they refuse to accept that this idealised object will never again light up their social experience. For supporters of the EDL, the rehabilitative work of mourning cannot yet begin.

Lost hope

The discourse of the melancholic acts to turn the subject away from social reality. Here, now, in the 21st century, there are few remaining cultures that have not been transformed, hollowed out, repackaged and rebranded by the insistent forces of capitalist globalisation. We now see the commodification of the 'traditional community' everywhere. This is not a process restricted to Africa, South America and other parts of the developing world. We already have museums and exhibitions dedicated to the English working class. This class is treated as a lost historical object, a thing of the past rather than the present. We can buy artefacts and keepsakes in the gift shop, and perhaps, before we head home, we can stop to listen to a group of student actors dressed up as miners, their faces smeared in soot, offer a stirring rendition of The Red Flag.

The reality is that this mythical community now exists only as a systematised form of identification that can be manipulated, commodified and exploited. The people who were once part of these cultures have now been thrust into the market as competitive individuals who must fight hard to secure wealth and prestige. They have been forced to accept a new reality in which the beauty of solidarity and duty to others are presented as fetters placed on the individual's freedom. The fraternal community has disappeared. Only competitive and insecure monadic market performers occupy contemporary capitalism's barren landscape; the hope, vitality, joy and security of the traditional community is but a warm and distant memory.

It is not just the English working class that has passed, and is passing, through this process. Ultimately all unique regional cultures will be subsumed by the market's expansionism. Only an insubstantial representation of the culture will remain. As time passes, we will become incapable of identifying the difference between the authentic community and its simulated representation. And, surrounded by the stupid pleasures of a hyper-mediatised consumer culture, we will have ceased to care.

Mourning the departed

In order to move forward, supporters of the EDL need to break through this cloud of melancholy so that the hard work of mourning can begin. The England these men seek to defend is already lost. The security and comforts of modern working-class community life have been destroyed. Its hidden rules and prohibitions, and it subtle inducements and transgressive pleasures, have melted into air. Only a cheap reproduction remains. An army of well-meaning middle-class sociologists and social policy experts remain absorbed in the myth of an active working-class consciousness and a deeply politicised community life. They leave no stone unturned in their desperate desire to locate somewhere in our most impoverished neighbourhoods organic egalitarian politics and a communal desire to resist capitalist expansionism. They project their liberal reformist political preferences on to the blank screen of social reality, and inevitably conclude that we are just one Labour government away from creating a new and progressive vibrancy in the decaying deindustrialised zones of the north. They steadfastly refuse to see the dark side, and they refuse to consciously acknowledge that, in their analysis of working-class community life, they are in fact inspecting a corpse.

Most men and women who live in these places tell very different stories. On many of the estates we visited, these stories are more and more inflected with anxiety, melancholy and an antagonism towards others. The energy that sustained the modern working-class community has drained away. Ultimately, our contacts seemed to know this. However, they were not yet capable of facing up to the pain that would accompany conscious acceptance of the truth. Instead, this knowledge continues to be repressed and forced back into the unconscious, where it evolves and mutates, and from where it casts its shadow on the emotions and activities of these homeless and redundant proletarians as they trudge through neighbourhoods beset by anxiety and conflict to their strip-lit workstations on characterless industrial estates at the edge of the city.

Mourning the departure of a love object is incredibly difficult, especially when that object has played a vital role in the creation and recreation of one's own social identity. However, it is only when we accept that our beloved is gone that we can begin to move forward with our lives. Our beloved is not forgotten, but we come to accept our beloved's non-existence in the present. The world supporters of the EDL hope to defend did not exist in the perfect form they imagine it, but, nonetheless, it was the source of their comfort and hope that cannot be brought back into existence.

However, while it may seem unlikely, it is still possible for the working class as a whole to discover, amid the detritus of neoliberalism, a new love object, someone or something that can reintroduce energy and passion to our lives. Rather than seek to defend an already dead community, it makes more sense to accept our loss and take stock of our transformed reality before beginning the process of creating new forms of security, satisfaction and recognition for ourselves and those we love – above all, a new basis for the return of the particular type of substantive hope that is vital to the spirit of the working class, and lies beyond the baseless optimism constantly forced on them and everyone else by the liberal middle class. This necessitates a return to politics.

A new love

Mourning the lost community, and rationally accepting its non-existence, has the potential to transform the social and political attitudes of the men we encountered during our prolonged investigation of the EDL. Accepting the truth of cultural breakdown and the atomisation of community would compel them to appraise the cold hard world of post-crash capitalism, and the faithless cynicism of postmodern experience. No one is formally excluded from consumer capitalism. All are invited to partake in its novelties, indulgences and commodified experiences. Capitalism today has no interest in the religion of the consumer. It has no interest in the ethnic backgrounds of those who strive to achieve success within its circuits. All are encouraged to compete, and all are encouraged to accept that anyone from any background has a chance to make it to the very top.

This, of course, is one of capitalism's fundamental attractions. Everyone, even those from the most marginalised backgrounds, are encouraged to believe that a dream life of consumer indulgence and hedonistic fulfilment could be theirs if they work hard or get lucky. The prizes on offer distract us from the stark fact that the overwhelming majority won't make it. Indeed, most don't even make it out of the starting gate.

Contemporary capitalism's expansive ideological support systems have achieved a supremacy never before seen in our history. We are all, like it or not, drawn into capitalism's ideological web. All unique cultures are ruthlessly commodified. Their inhabitants are deprived of the security of their traditional communities and told to make a go of it in an increasingly dog-eat-dog world in which there is progressively less concern for the losers. Perhaps immigrant communities are better able to put up some initial resistance, but they are themselves only a generation or two from atomisation and absorption into the competitive capitalist milieu.

If our contacts were to accept that their lost community is totally lost, then the truth of their present reality can be revealed and consciously accepted. However, accepting the death of their community and the total triumph of liberal capitalism need not feed into the cynicism and pragmatism that already exists in such abundance today. It is still possible to fight to create something better, and, if the left can revive the special substantive hope to create a world less scarred by injustice, it needs the working class to return to politics with an absolutely steadfast determination to dispense with the forces that have for the past two centuries been destroying traditional cultures and secure ways of life.

Quite clearly, the sense of security, comfort and repose these men once found in their communities is anathema in liberal capitalism's new global order. Acceptance of the permanent disappearance of the traditional community would encourage our contacts to look liberal capitalism square in the face, and this shocking encounter might then force them to think anew about their structural position as consumers and units of labour, and the inherent injustices of global political economy. From that point we might imagine that it becomes possible to develop a very different politics, a politics that reflects and acknowledges the atomisation and instrumentality of our times, and acts to close the gap between the subject and its other in order to manufacture a way of living together that is less hostile, less distant, less competitive, and from which new forms of mutual recognition and respect might emerge. This acceptance of a troubling reality opens up the possibility that global capitalism can again be identified as the true enemy of a working class that has freed itself from the compulsions of competitive individualism, and can once again see the necessity of solidarity and togetherness.

Ultimately, it was the profit motive that destroyed the communities in which our contacts once lived, and it is the profit motive that has made their working lives competitive, insecure and anxiety-inducing. There are a range of important associated issues, but this is the truth of the matter. If the working class can accept a new vanguard, and if the profit motive can again be problematised by the political representatives of the working class, then it is possible this class can again establish itself as a political force in England. If this series of events were to come to pass, our political culture would very quickly burst back into life, and British society would be in a position to imagine a different world, one built on a firm commitment to the inclusion, recognition and wellbeing of all.

Accepting this reality also opens up the possibility that a new and meaningful community life might be brought into existence that reflects our present reality. This new community would be firmly rooted in the here and now. It would be forced to constitute itself as a political community, and its members would quickly realise that differences based on religion and skin colour are relatively insignificant when placed alongside the epochal problems we face now, and those problems that await us in the near future. A new politics of universality, a politics that cuts across the social field to create new forms of attachment, community and recognition, is quite clearly the most progressive route forwards. The 'tolerance of difference' must take a back seat, and the acknowledgement and acceptance of sameness must come to the fore. Only a new politics of universalism can prevent a gradual drift towards internecine ethnic and religious hostility, and only a new politics of universalism can equip us with the political and intellectual tools we will need to defend civil society, in all its social and ethnic diversity, from the forces about to be unleashed by the continued acceleration of climate change.

Death and dying in the EDL

When asked about the leadership and organisation of the EDL, many of our contacts said that they were reasonably content with its messy structure and its imprecise goals. They didn't want a leader. They tended to believe that a leader would, inevitably, let them down in some way. In offering this kind of assessment, they found themselves constrained by the debilitating cynicism of our times. Postmodernism has, since the 1980s, relieved us of our fervent beliefs. We have been encouraged to assume that every cause is flawed in some important respect. Every political movement is potentially tyrannical. Every leader is a potential despot out to advance her own interests. Every religion is simply a complicated creation myth that forcibly turns its adherents away from reality.

These days it seems that there is nothing pure left for us to believe in. This cynicism and lack of faith is closely related to our total faith in our own infallible logic and rationality. The only thing we truly believe in is our own lack of belief, and the power of our critical faculties to identify and avoid the bullshit that lies strewn across the fields of politics, society and culture. More than at any point in history, we believe that we see the world as it truly is. We are sceptical of all truth claims, and over the course of many years, we have become increasingly sceptical that there is indeed an unsullied truth capable of capturing our hearts.

All this means that we cynically dismiss new political movements that come along now and then with the promise of improving our societies. We assume that, in the fullness of time, we will be let down in some way, and because of this we refuse to join in, or else we offer only half-hearted support, usually from the comfort of an armchair. We assume that the leader, who at the moment talks passionately about, for example, curbing capitalism's excesses, redistributing income and returning to the old principle of full employment, will be revealed as a self-interested careerist, someone who was, all along, out to grab what he could for himself. Or we assume that the leader is a power-hungry narcissist, and that all of his momentarily alluring platitudes will count for nothing if he ever manages to win power. This obdurate cynicism has had a debilitating effect on our culture, and its dominance of the political field meant that the EDL, like any other political movement, was always destined to fail.

From the outset the EDL has been without clear leadership. Tommy Robinson seemed for a time to be its leader, but in reality he had little control over the movement or the men who headed out on to the streets to support it. The movement developed in a ramshackle manner. It grew without too much forethought and planning. The rise of the EDL was not orchestrated by identifiable leaders or by shady powers behind the scenes. Its focus on the problems they imagined were caused by Muslims attracted support, and before those involved knew it, the EDL had very quickly become a political movement of national significance. But it had no identifiable hierarchy or organisation. Regional groups simply got on with it and did what they could to draw attention to their concerns. They were not managed by a centralised body keen to ensure ideological purity and adherence to strategy. There was no intellectual vanguard feeding the movement with ideas. The EDL produced no manifesto, no clear policies, and it made no overtures towards the main political parties. There was little by way of strategy. The movement had no goals, and no clear image existed of what success for the EDL would look like. All that existed was a basic desire to challenge the place of Muslims in English society, and to reduce the numbers of immigrants coming in to the country. But how would these goals be realised? No one seemed to know. For the men who protested, this didn't really matter. They were simply registering their dissatisfaction. They were keen to communicate their message to the rest of the country, and they would do it their way. They wouldn't be led around by a bunch of preening would-be politicians.

Some of those we talked to recognised quite early on that it would be almost impossible for the movement to make genuine progress. A lack of organisation and the absence of a clear and realistic plan to influence politics would eventually mean that interest waned and numbers dwindled. How would doing the same thing over and over again – protesting in the street and campaigning on the internet – push the movement forward? Generally speaking, our contacts appeared to yearn for a powerful leader who would establish clear goals and set about the task of realising them, an orator to take the reins and begin the task of attracting others to the movement. Quite clearly, they wanted the EDL to grow. They wanted politicians to listen to their message.

Many said they were happy simply to turn up from time to time to disrupt and disturb the liberal mainstream. They liked upsetting people. They liked offending shoppers out on a

Saturday afternoon, and they hated the anti-fascists who turned up at their demos with their placards and megaphones. The old atmosphere of the football away-day remained. Lager, cocaine, a bit of shouting and singing, the possibility of a punch-up, surrounded by friends and like-minded others – there was an air of adventure to proceedings, and some found all of this very attractive. Others were a little more sober and serious about the EDL's cause, and, despite the attractions of a carnivalesque day on the drink, everyone we spoke to was quite clearly worried about the effects of Muslim immigration, and angry about the gradual erasure of English culture and tradition.

They wanted to get their message across, and they didn't care whether the liberal mainstream found their message offensive. They wanted those in power to know that they were pissed off and that they weren't going to sit back and take it anymore. Most of those we spoke to at demos cited this as their most powerful conscious motivation. Some spoke of their desire to recruit others to the cause, but a simple urge to communicate their anger was paramount. However, as we discussed these issues with our contacts it became clear that many of those actively involved in the movement wanted much more than this. They couldn't trust a leader, but they wanted their activism to mean something. They wanted to win a tangible victory, and they wanted to put an end to Muslim immigration to the UK.

Debilitating cynicism

The movement developed, and then declined, in an era in which we show remarkably little faith in our political leaders. We have already seen that the emergence of organic working-class symbolic systems, intellectuals and leaders has been suppressed by liberal middle-class elites for over a hundred years. In the neoliberal era postmodernism arose to promise what liberals hoped would be the final destruction of the very idea that a heroic leader capable of inspiring and unifying a nation could yet again arise. The upside is that we avoid the vortex of death and destruction into which we have been led in the past. But the downside is that we remain marooned in the depressing neoliberal doldrums now characterised by growing inequality (see Harvey, 2011; Piketty, 2014; Dorling, 2015), and a diverse range of insecurities and unresolved antagonisms (Winlow and Hall, 2013; Horsley, 2015).

Thus we continue with our half-hearted efforts to regulate what is, fobbing off the population with the deliberate conflation of regulation and reform, fetishistically disavowing our knowledge that the two are not the same. We can regulate capitalism and curb some of its excesses, but capitalism cannot be 'reformed' – once we lift the regulation, even for a moment, the system begins to revert to its brutal origin.

In this hiatus politics has lost much of its ideological substance. It can offer no real hope. Politics has collapsed into biopolitics, the administration of what already exists, a secular ministerium that must maintain its own credibility by preventing too much articulate empathy with those who suffer the worst excesses of redundancy and marginality. The only goals our politicians openly commit to these days are cheerleading the expansion of consumer lifestyles, maintaining the population's basic physical health and protecting the nation from external threats. The utopian drive to create in reality something fundamentally better than what currently exists has no place in contemporary parliamentary politics. Since 2008 even these goals are difficult to identify in manifestos and political speeches.

In these times of soul-crushing neoliberal pragmatism all the grand ideals of modern politics appear quaint and simplistic. There is no future for us to move towards. There is simply a commitment to reproduce the present in the least disruptive way. But this carries its own risk. To remain as we are, lodged in this depressive intervallic period – to do nothing and change nothing – is to risk slow-motion social disintegration. Advances in technology and automation, combined with the relocation of production centres to the east, will very soon render the majority of the post-industrial west's population marginal to the productive economy. Inarticulate awareness of that process of gradual disintegration will be felt first and most acutely on the expanding margins, where, if the left remains trapped in liberalism's cage, many individuals will continue to fantasise about a strong leader of the right who promises to set matters straight.

EIGHT

Conclusion: Why the left must begin from the beginning again

In this book we have spent some considerable time addressing the transformation of the mainstream political left. For us it is clear that the rise of the right in the 21st century is inextricably connected to the decline of the left as a serious political force.

Since the 1970s the left has stumbled from defeat to defeat to defeat. Today's relentless conservative and liberal media attacks on Jeremy Corbyn's new opposition, salvo after salvo fired out of every position across the spectrum, from *The Sun* to *The Guardian*, threaten the left's fragile revival among the young. Today, more young people feel empathy with those suffering on the margins because, in neoliberalism's insecure economy, they can sense that there is a genuine chance they might join them there. The economic insecurity long experienced by the old industrial proletariat is spreading throughout the social body. Many young people will start their careers in insecure and poorly paid service sector jobs. Even for graduates this is true. And with the passage of time, fewer young people are progressing into more secure and better paid work. The labour markets they hoped to enter have been exposed to job insecurity. There is little left that can be relied on. Perennial insecurity is now perfectly normal. Unless the left can engage the people in a meaningful discussion about how these stark problems can be addressed, and how the economy might be reorganised with a view to making it work for the majority of citizens, it is staring yet another defeat in the face. A yet more destructive era of neoliberal pragmatism will begin. Asset stripping will continue and hard-won entitlements will be withdrawn. All of modernity's partial achievements will begin to break apart and crumble into the dust of history. Anger will continue to grow, and things will become tougher and tougher for ordinary men and women across the country.

The neoliberal right has achieved total ideological domination of the field of political economy, and the power and influence of reactionary right-wing populism is growing day by the day. For the most part, the left has withdrawn from the lifeworlds of the working class, and it no longer wages war to improve the lifestyles and security of the proletariat at the expense of those who have amassed staggering wealth as a result of ongoing economic restructuring. A variety of attempts are currently underway to reconnect with those in the west who suffer most from the tyranny of markets. But, unfortunately, those engaged in this process are marginal to the mainstream democratic left's current political project, and continue to be cast into the wilderness by the mass media's relentless demonisation.

The left lost interest in the traditional fight to effect genuine change on the field of political economy, and instead opened up new theatres of conflict on the field of culture. Generally speaking, the left accepted the capitalist horizon. Instead of attempting to restrain capitalism's tendency towards socially destructive profit-seeking, the left set about the ceaseless task of attempting to disperse rights a little more evenly within the system as it stands. The left's current activity on the field of culture and identity politics covers up a deeper inactivity. It has abandoned the field of political economy almost entirely, the field on which we must focus if true progress is to be made. Old slogans about 'changing the world without taking power' now seem quite ridiculous, and serve only to assure the neoliberal power bloc that the left is now entirely domesticated, and remind those trapped in the margins that it is too weak and divided to function on their behalf.

We do not deny that the radical liberalism of the 1960s pushed the left in new and interesting directions, but each one of these directions took the left further and further away from the working class. Let's be clear about this: the left's abandonment of the fundamental commitment to class struggle – and its gradual drift towards divisive identity politics – has been an utter disaster. And it has been an utter disaster for all of us.

The liberalisation of the left, and its consequences

As we have tried to show, what the left needs now isn't a project that stops at the point of encouraging all to respect diversity or tolerate difference. Our job as academics is not to scan the horizon in the hope of identifying some new micro community that deserves our sympathy. Philanthropy is not enough. At this point in our history we need something more forceful. We need to overcome the deadlock of contemporary politics, and we need to construct and popularise a vision of a future socioeconomic system in which all are included in both participation and outcomes by right, and in which the obscene divisions and injustices of contemporary neoliberalism are completely absent. The first step is to ditch our obsession with personal freedom and reassert our commitment to the common good.

Those who argue that cultural intolerance must be positioned at the core of the left's political agenda cover up with their beautiful, multicoloured liberal cloak a fundamental and very ugly class antagonism that must now be exposed and discussed. We have grown used to talking about toleration, but rarely now do we talk about exploitation , and we never talk about systemic exploitation at all. This should strike us as odd. Our economic system continues to rest on exploitation. It is not as if we can say that we have successfully overcome exploitation, and the only task that now lies in front of the left is the cultivation of a more tolerant cultural order.

Many on the liberal left express sympathy for the poor, and many are committed to providing the poor with better welfare services. However, some of this group display a marked distaste for the working class as a whole and what they perceive to be the conservativism and intolerance that demean their cultures. The poor are welcomed to the liberal left's ongoing political project, but only on the condition that they ditch for good any vestigial class and cultural commitments they may carried with them. Everyone on the left today must be tolerant and liberal. Those who aren't tolerant and liberal are the enemy, even if they are in desperate need of assistance and political representation, and form part of a social group that has been systematically exploited by our economic system for centuries.

Our contacts often appeared to sense the liberal left's thinly veiled fear and loathing of the disreputable white working class, and it infuriated them enormously. What are we to make of this situation, where the left line up against those elements of the working class whose reactionary bile is reproduced and intensified by the left's unwillingness to fight on the field of political economy? Why do the left's representatives in Parliament steadfastly refuse to even talk about class? Why is there not a leftist commitment to the interests of the working class as such, in all of its real-world diversity? This commitment is unlikely to arise among an institutional old left that believes we are all middle class now, or a cultural new left that sees class as only one relation – and in many cases, the least important – in the intersectional matrix.

The liberalisation of the left, and the dominance of the middle class within it, played a direct and significant role in our contacts' adoption of right-wing nationalism, creating it anew, or persuading them by means of its cowardly withdrawal from political economy to renew their subscription to reactionary ideas that still hang in the air. They hated the contemporary left's weird, destructive and effete counter-culturalism, and could discern no connection whatsoever between the left and England's proletarian class. They believed that they were viewed by the left as vulgar barbarians, and it was clear to them that the left was totally disinterested in the significant and very real problems they faced. This contempt created not simply a 'self-fulfilling prophecy', but a means by which the liberalised left vicariously fulfilled someone else's prophecy on their behalf – namely, the conservative right. We should recognise that this destructive relational sentiment is not new – self-proclaimed 'socialist' Lady Shaw once revealed that she would be happy for the working class to run the country as long as she wouldn't have to invite any of them round for tea.

The liberalised middle-class left, supporters of the EDL believed, had become the principal enemy of the English working class. The left cared far more about immigrants and people with different sexual proclivities than it did about its own manual class, the class of people who emptied their bins, delivered their pizzas, serviced their cars and fixed their boilers, the class of people who had been the nation's factory and cannon fodder throughout history. For us, the left today needs to be returned to the working class. Its key representatives should be members of the working class. It is the working class that must win the fight for social and economic justice. Middle-class liberals cannot and will not win it on their behalf.

When our contacts spoke about the election of Jeremy Corbyn to the leadership of the Labour Party, they did not speak of the return of genuine choice at election time. They did not compare social democracy to liberal democracy, and they did not talk about the pros and cons associated with the state taking a more active role in the formal economy. They did not even attempt to calculate which of the main political parties would best represent their economic interests. There were no expansive conversations about nationalisation or the implications of a new governmental commitment to tax wealth to a greater extent. These were everyday men and women in insecure and often demeaning work with pressing practical commitments and concerns. They were not intellectuals and did not aspire to be so. The truth is that they saw Jeremy Corbyn as a do-gooding, weak-as-piss hippy pacifist. They did not see a leader with the potential to upset the existing order of things. They saw only continuity in Corbyn, the continuity of a system that undervalued them and people like them, and the continuity of a long-running process of gradual decline. They saw someone who cared more about the welfare of migrants than about the old proletariat, and they hated him. What does this hatred of Jeremy Corbyn tell us? To suggest that these men are simply atavistic Neanderthals incapable of identifying an obvious truth tells us nothing and avoids the central issue. Something much more important is going on here, and it is something the left needs to pay attention to in the years ahead.

The Blair and Brown years were an absolute disaster for the left. The cultural new left had long been written off as generally useless, unelectable and in many ways actively counter-productive to their interests. But during these years it became progressively easier for members of the working class to see that even the institutional left that named itself as the party of labour had little interest in protecting and advancing their interests. The decades of deindustrialisation and mass immigration impacted on the lives of the white working class in ways that the middle-class liberals who had taken control of the Labour Party fail to acknowledge or appreciate. Labour's staunch advocacy of multiculturalism and high levels of immigration, combined with its inability to reverse deindustrialisation and return tenured labour and economic security to working-class regions, encouraged many in the white working class to feel that they were on the bottom of everyone's list. As New Labour pressed on with its plan to reinvigorate the party and make it appealing to an electorate concerned mostly about income growth and standards of living, it became increasingly difficult to see any representatives from the working class operating in important positions in the Westminster bubble.

What we see here is not simply the reduction of the Labour Party's political capital in areas dominated by the white working class. Rather, Labour's problem became the left's problem. The anger was such that it was applied indiscriminately, and the entirety of the left was tarnished in the eyes of a significant number of white working-class men and women. The rise of right-wing populism in those areas most affected by deindustrialisation is not simply a random contingency thrown up by the movement of history and reproduced by existing 'narratives' and 'discourses' that can be 'subverted' and remade in the ethereal realm of symbols. These two processes are closely connected and firmly grounded in the real and harmful consequences of neoliberalism's politically driven tectonic shift in the global economy.

We have tried throughout the book to communicate the sense of sadness and anger that exists in England's white working-class neighbourhoods. There we found little to suggest that progress might be just a little further along the road. It pained us greatly to see these proletarians marching under the flag of fascism. However, when our contacts told us that they had been abandoned and could see no vocal advocate to speak for them on the field of politics, we were forced to agree. In their various ways our contacts seemed to know that in recent years politics had taken a profound middle-class liberal turn, and that people like them had to adapt to this new reality or die out. They were unable to adapt, and they did not want to die out. Instead they kicked out at those they believed had caused their suffering and those who threatened to eradicate the last vestiges of their culture and community. This is the uncomfortable reality the left must now be bold enough to face up to.

The rise of the right

Throughout Europe right-wing populism has grown to the extent that we can now legitimately begin to think about the very real possibility of a fascist future. The new right-wing nationalism will not be a carbon copy of 20th-century European fascism, but fascism it will be, nonetheless. For years this seemed unthinkable. It seemed that we were together becoming increasingly liberal and tolerant of difference in a social democratic continuum that would guide us all into a bright future. The triumph of western liberalism has ensured the return of its own opposite. These two – fascism and liberalism – are bound together. Each actively assists the other to evolve within and across distinct historical contexts. Liberalism's ostensible victory on the fields of culture, politics and economics has fomented the growth of opposition groups fully committed to the dismissal of liberalism's shallow freedoms and the retrieval of supposedly authentic traditions, cultures and ways of life. Groups like the EDL appear quite marginal at the moment, but nationalist parties have already taken power elsewhere in Europe, and nationalist movements are growing all the time.

We should expect this process to continue. Climate change will inevitably lead to growing numbers of people making their way to parts of the world less damaged by the ecological transformation. Around the equator, in the Tropical Convergence Zone where whole agricultural systems are being destroyed by long periods of drought punctuated by huge random flash floods, it is becoming harder and harder to sustain life. State governance is breaking down and violence is rising (Parenti, 2011). Huge numbers of people are moving north – and in the process, abandoning their cultures and traditions – in the hope that they might find something better for themselves and their children. Many more have been displaced by wars and incessant cultural and political conflict (UNHCR, 2015). And where do they hope to go? Where would you hope to go? The spectacle of western affluence inevitably draws the attention of those forced to leave their homes behind, and as millions migrate across land and sea in the hope of finally arriving at a destination that promises to put an end to their suffering, a destination that promises peace, stability, employment, welfare and order, those who already live precarious lives in the west's deindustrialised zones begin to worry. And their worries grow. Increased inward migration will drive the formation of Europe's new nationalist movements at an even faster pace. That much is clear. The EDL appears to be splintering and shrinking slightly, and UKIP are not advancing at quite the rate one might have predicted, but the Conservative and Labour parties appear to have got the message that the people want an end to inward migration. And what of the new populist nationalist movements in Germany, in France, across Scandinavia and the Benelux countries, and throughout much of Eastern Europe?

How can the left begin to work through these problems? Ultimately, it needs to shed its skin and become something else entirely. We must recognise that the adoption of hippy counter-culturalism was a colossal error, and then begin to repair some of the damage it has caused. The first step is to reconnect with the working class with a renewed order of grounded universal ethics and truthful symbolism comprehensible to all cultural groups. We must dispense with the liberal-postmodernist dictum that there is no privileged truth and each cellular cultural group is entitled to generate its own – the EDL's beliefs ride on the back of this principle – and renew a multipolar dialectic grounded in socioeconomic reality. Culture must not be abandoned but put back in its sub-dominant place, and on the field of politics the multicultural must become the transcultural. The broad working class exist at the epicentre of this reality, and remain absolutely integral to progressive politics. We must use our educational institutions to inform the working class truthfully of the forces that created their present difficulties and of the future that lies ahead. We must do this in such a way that allows the working class to re-educate and re-politicise itself from the position it has experienced and can readily comprehend, and then we must place the renewed politics of the working class at the very core of the left. We must do all we can to jolt the people out of their cynicism and resignation. We must fight to redirect the anger of the people towards the true cause of their insecurity and suffering.

In the midst of such intellectual dynamism the left can be rehabilitated. Reconnecting with the working class and persuading them to believe in its project is a very difficult task, but it can be done. Preventing right-wing populism from advancing still further also seems very difficult. We have already passed key climate tipping points (Barnosky and Hardly, 2016), resource wars are being fought around the globe (Klare, 2001), and large corporations and global superpowers are planning for a bleak future in which climate change and mass migration prompt the collapse of national economies and threaten the continuity of civil society (Parenti, 2011). Perhaps the pessimists are correct. Perhaps we will need to pass through a powerful historic shock before things can change. Or perhaps we can rediscover the power of belief and a dogged determination to join with others to prevent the disaster that awaits us just a little further along the road.

Postscript: Brexit and working-class politics

We wrote the majority of this book in 2015. Our project was at an end by the time the nation went to the polls in June 2016 to vote on Britain's continued membership of the European Union. Roughly 52% of those who voted wanted to bring Britain's membership to an end. More than 33.5 million people voted in the referendum, and almost 17.5 million people voted to leave. Most columnists, commentators, pundits and broadcasters – and the enlightened liberals who dominate our academic institutions – were shocked by the result. They just could not understand how and why so many voters had been persuaded by the fearmongering of the Leave campaign. How could voters place their trust in Nigel Farage, Boris Johnson and Michael Gove? These men represented the elite, and they were committed to ensuring the continued dominance of capital over human life. Couldn't people see this? How could so many voters fall for the absurd claims the elite made about the economic benefits of leaving? Didn't these voters find the Leave campaign's blatant demonisation of immigrants distasteful? Didn't they know that the EU generally benefits Britain's economy, and that a vote to leave the EU was a vote for economic uncertainty and a reduction in living standards for the majority?

The economy did indeed enter a period of crisis immediately after the result was announced. As we write these words the road ahead remains uncertain. The great fear of ongoing economic turmoil – a fear lodged permanently in the British psyche after almost 40 years of neoliberalism – now frames the pious soul-saving of those whose job it is to promote a progressive liberal worldview that seeks, but hopelessly fails, to mitigate the social, economic, cultural and personal disasters free market capitalism has wreaked on the western world.

It quickly became clear that many of those who occupy the nation's dead and decaying deindustrialised zones had voted to leave. This prompted the beautiful souls of the metropole to begin their own process of demonisation. The atavistic white working class were too stupid to recognise their own economic best interests, and they seemed to be dedicated to the task of tearing down all the towering achievements of multiculturalism. Didn't they see the great benefits of cultural diversity? How could they not be sympathetic towards the millions of people who had left their countries of origin to journey thousands of miles in search of something better?

The nation was in the grip of a new and virulent form of racism, the liberal commentariat claimed, and regressive elements among the old white working class were its driving force. Guileless proletarians had been duped by career politicians who had played on and exacerbated an extant cultural antagonism towards the non-white population. There can be no excuses for racism. The sources, reproductive cultures and incidents of such idiotic bigotry need to be challenged at once and held to account. The white working class, quite clearly, had fallen victim to dark forces keen to stir up racism and xenophobia. A new age of stupidity and blind prejudice was beginning to emerge. Now was the time for the forces of light, civility and progress to mount a determined fightback against the forces of darkness. Every weapon available should be called on.

In the midst of this national soul-searching many headed out on to the streets to take part in impromptu demonstrations against the Brexit vote, especially in London. The initial sense of shock endured. Now, almost a month after the vote, there is still, in the broadsheet press and across the mainstream media, a palpable sense of wonder and disbelief. Why had Britain decided to act against its own best interests? What inspired this weird form of national self-flagellation? Could it all have been just a colossal mistake? Should the government ignore the majority, fudge around Article 50, and remain?

Everyone in the mainstream media's orbit seemed to have voted to remain. Those journalists whose words we read in national newspapers, and whose voices we hear on television and radio, remain a relatively privileged occupational group, and they belong to the educated metropolitan middle class. This group, we now know, voted overwhelmingly to stay in the EU. But the contact these journalists had with the white working classes of the north and Wales was close to non-existent. They know very little about the social, political and economic realities that shaped the lives of those who voted to leave. Occasionally, a voice from the provinces, usually a man or women stopped by a TV reporter while out shopping somewhere up north, would intrude on the genteel world of broadcast media and state bluntly that they were fed up with immigration and wanted an end to it. Of course, before the referendum these isolated voices had usually been framed by a subtle narrative that sought to remind viewers – who, it was assumed were broadly liberal, educated and pragmatic – that a few numbskulls still prevailed out there in the wastelands of the north. Now, after the referendum, the liberal commentariat has discovered that there were, in fact, many millions of people out there who felt the same. The division seemed obvious: enlightened progressives versus fearful and economically illiterate white racists. The nation appeared to have been torn asunder by what had at first appeared to be a rather dull referendum about Britain's continued membership of a pan-continental union geared towards boosting economic growth and trade between neighbouring states. Somehow the referendum had managed to engage the people in the way that general elections these days appeared unable to do. How are we to make sense of it all?

The return of the silent majority

The silent majority had momentarily stirred, asserted its will, and then returned immediately to its slumber, and the liberal commentariat had to respond quickly to the unexpected result. Optimism was at a premium. All indications suggested things would get worse, and they would get worse for everybody. Someone or something needed to be identified, blamed and then thoroughly castigated. The white working class – who, generally speaking, had not benefited from a higher education and who still appeared to be attached to a range of regressive attitudes and beliefs – were the obvious culprit.

It was clear that social class was a vital part of the story, but there were other notable aspects. The young, it transpired, had voted overwhelmingly to stay in the EU (see Elgot, 2016; Cosslett, 2016a, b). Older populations had voted to leave. The same kinds of reductive logic, absurd generalisation and bilious mischaracterisation began to appear in the comment sections of the broadsheet press. Apparently the young were forward-looking, open, better-educated and totally dedicated to multiculturalism, whereas the old were poorly educated racists who had milked the welfare system and lived through a time of historic prosperity. The older population, apparently, didn't care that from now on the younger generation would not have it so good. They were more concerned with their own prejudices than with the economic wellbeing of the young and the country at large. The best thing they could do was die off and let the young get on with the task of correcting their mistakes. Underneath this predictable rhetoric, however, a range of submerged antagonisms that had been building throughout the neoliberal epoch were beginning to surface; careful, nuanced and revealing analyses were thin on the ground.

Quickly many began to demand that the government should not act on the result. There was no constitutional reason why the government must invoke Article 50 and begin the process of leaving the EU. Stories quickly began to appear in the press suggesting that millions now regretted their decision to vote to leave. They had been conned by the Leave campaign, they didn't realise the importance of the vote, and they had failed to fully consider the economic implications of exiting the EU. Some commentators, especially those on the political right, suggested that the government should use the result to secure a better deal from the EU – especially with regard to curtailing the flow of economic migrants from mainland Europe into Britain – without leaving the union entirely. Others suggested that a general election should be called, and that enacting the Leave vote should be made central to campaigning. Stories of falling house prices, mass unemployment, tumbling share prices and 'lost generations' were everywhere (see, for example, Fraser, 2016; Rodionova, 2016; Vale, 2016; Wearden and Fletcher, 2016).

The result of the referendum might have shocked the liberal commentariat, but it certainly didn't shock us. Anyone with any recent first-hand experience of the old working class's precarious existence and hardening attitudes must have seen this coming (see also McKenzie, 2016). We work in the university sector, and most of our colleagues across the country were convinced that the Remain campaign would win the day. Remain had the best arguments. It had the more intelligent and persuasive supporters from the fields of politics, culture and mass media. Of course, many academics are deeply and unshakeably attached to logic and rationality. They believed that the people would vote for the campaign that presented the strongest case, and the strongest case, quite clearly, belonged to Remain. It was clear that economic turmoil would result if the nation voted to leave the EU. Everyone would be worse off, and this, surely, would be the determining factor. However, 'logic' and 'rationality' are always tied to ideology. Many of our colleagues simply couldn't see the festering sores and open wounds of those sections of British society that had suffered the worst effects of neoliberal restructuring. When you have almost nothing to lose, when you can see nothing positive on the horizon, and when you're convinced that you have been betrayed and cast aside, 'logic' and 'rationality' cannot remain dominant. For many of those struggling by on low incomes after decades of EU membership and liberalism's promises, it was 'logical' to do the only thing that stood even a remote chance of substantively improving their immediate circumstances.

Academics and journalists tend to be middle class and reasonably affluent, and because people who are affluent and middle class tend to live among others who are affluent and middle class, it seemed clear to them that Remain would romp to a convincing victory. Everyone seemed to agree that remaining in the EU was clearly the best course of action. Some even hoped that the impending victory would give our political leaders a mandate to pursue greater economic and political integration with our European neighbours. For them, the vote was about embracing diversity, and making it clear that the racists at the margins would not succeed with their divisive project. The overwhelming majority of our colleagues hate UKIP, and they hate what UKIP represents. They are happy for the nation to accept more refugees and more economic migrants, and they hope to lend their support to political movements that seek to overcome the prejudices of new anti-immigrant political groups. If everything went to plan, a positive result in the referendum could herald the dawning of a new age of multicultural vibrancy and toleration.

If only more academics had left the leafy confines of the campus – and the comfortable, friendly and sedate neighbourhoods in which they tend to live – and headed out in to the real world to meet real people and discuss with them the pressures and frustrations they face in their everyday lives, they would have seen that out there in the provinces things are trending downwards. More and more people, less 'resilient' than some believe, feel helpless, forgotten, ignored and cut adrift from the mainstream. You can afford to be reasonably positive about the future when you have a reasonable wage and an ongoing stake in civil society. The future doesn't look quite so rosy when you're plagued by debt, and when your job is insecure and poorly paid. If you don't know how you'll pay the rent next month, or how you'll afford to feed your family, optimism recedes and darker emotions come to the fore.

Anger and frustration are everywhere these days. The truth of the matter is that we don't have to look too far to find these things. Social scientists in particular should have seen this coming. Huge numbers of people want change in a system that has outlawed the very idea of change. They don't see themselves as beneficiaries of our economic and cultural systems. They feel locked out and undervalued, assailed by constant frustrations and pressures. As the years go by things appear to be getting tougher and tougher. Unable to change track, they want the track to change, to lead somewhere better. They want to put an end to the pressures they face. They feel they deserve something better. Of course, change is not offered to the people at election time. The choice between neoliberals in red ties and neoliberals in blue ties just doesn't cut it. All mainstream political parties offer more of the same. But here, with the Brexit vote, people could sense an opportunity to display their dissatisfaction with what the country had become, and where it appeared to be going.

Ultimately, the 17.5 million people who voted to leave the EU were voting for change as such. Any change would do, because there was nothing in the question posed to the electorate that was truly positive and forward-looking. People could vote to stay in a union totally committed to the continuation of free market capitalism, the primary financial institutions of which have enforced destructive austerity policies across the continent. In particular, the EU has recently compelled southern states, especially Greece, to withdraw welfare and social services in the hope of balancing the books. The human costs of this strategy have been enormous. Alternatively, people could vote to leave. This would inevitably destabilise the economy, reduce employment and in all likelihood, without the various mechanisms of the EU to keep the rapacious corporate sector in check, usher in a new age of pure market domination. Neither outcome augured well. The referendum seemed to follow the established parameters of domesticated democratic politics by limiting voters to the opportunity to endorse the political party they disliked the least.

On balance, it appears that the British population would have been marginally better off if they had decided to stay in the EU. Most academics and journalists, and many educated Remain voters, could see this, and they voted in accordance with their own economic self-interest. Their cultural preferences also played a part. Remain voters, generally speaking, were against the racism of UKIP, and against all of the assumed prejudices of those who hoped to reduce immigration. They recognised the benefits of immigration and cultural diversity, and hoped to present an open and welcoming aspect to the rest of the civilised world. However, many of those who live in the deindustrialised zones of Wales and the north of England couldn't see any economic benefit in remaining in the EU. The country had been in the EU for some time, yet for them things had got progressively worse.

How could things get worse still? How? Many of those we spoke to worked very hard for terrible rates of pay. Their jobs were insecure and they were cut adrift from mainstream civil society. They knew that all the glittering prizes of consumer society would in all likelihood remain out of reach. Their neighbourhoods were disorderly and unkempt, and they knew beyond doubt that if things continued on as they were, their sons and daughters would fare even worse. The economic benefits of remaining in the EU? What benefits? When would these benefits trickle down to the ordinary men and women who struggled to make ends meet? Things had been getting progressively worse for decades. The oft-discussed account of the economic benefits of remaining in the EU simply had no purchase among groups that had already experienced a significant reduction in their incomes and status. When members of these groups were told it would be easier to get a job if Britain remained in the EU, they were understandably cynical and dismissive about yet another false promise. The status quo had offered them absolutely nothing. The jobs that were available were of the very worst kind. No. They wanted out. They wanted change. They wanted something, anything, that wasn't this. They would use their vote to register their dissatisfaction, and hope against hope that life outside the EU, under the full democratic control of the British electorate with no outside interference, would provide them with something better.

All this was tied up with the thorny issue of immigration. It was assumed by many that if the country voted to leave the EU, fewer immigrants would enter the country. There is also some truth in the suggestion that some Leave voters hoped that the result would enable politicians to expel immigrants already in the country, and generally act to reduce the cultural and ethnic diversity of multicultural Britain. As we noted above, many commentators suggested that the drive to cut immigration, which we now know is quite common throughout the country, referenced a new and virulent form of postmodern racism rooted in hatred and fear. However, for us as academics this is all a little too easy. We believe that new forms of cultural enmity are on the rise. Throughout our research we witnessed this reality. There are certainly some locales in which it is now perfectly normal to hear talk of the problems caused by immigrants and, as we document throughout the book, it is Muslims who tend to bear the brunt of this.

New forms of bigotry and intolerance appear to be emerging, but why? It's easy to say that you are 'against racism'. It's easy to say that racism is wrong and that it must be opposed. However, for us it seems important to dig beneath contemporary racism in the hope of discovering where it comes from and why it takes its current form. Only when we understand what we oppose will we be in a position to challenge and overcome it. Why, at this point in our history, are so many people so keen to cut immigration? Why is there such hostility towards Muslim immigrants in particular? How have such views taken root, and what other issues might be at stake?

We believe we have offered in these pages an easily accessible account of some of most important issues, even some tentative answers to the questions they beg. We have tried to ditch as much academic obscurantism, and go straight to the heart of the matter. We have focused on the most extreme expressions of white working–class nationalism, but, we think, our analysis can also illuminate growing fear of and hostility towards otherness among the broad white working class. For many ordinary working people, growing diversity and continued inward migration is inextricably bound up with the context of their own declining fortunes. For them, migrants are first and foremost economic competitors. They make it harder to get and keep a job, and they place downward pressure on wage levels. This narrative springs from the experience of ordinary white working men and women, and it acts as a foundation for the forms of cultural enmity that develop in relation to it.

Many readers will be able to recognise that this narrative oversimplifies the economic issues at stake. However, it is the immediate experience of those struggling at the bottom that matters most. Their experience tells them that it would be easier to get and keep a job if millions of recently arrived migrants were somewhere else, and not competing in the same labour markets. Talk of the overall net economic benefits of high levels of immigration cuts no ice. People struggling by on low incomes simply don't care about the contribution of immigrant populations to the nation's GDP. Understandably enough, they see such debates as a distraction, and a way of avoiding any discussion of the impact immigration has had on particular labour markets and particular locales. Macro-level analysis doesn't tell us much about how things play out at a local level, or about rising levels of competition in the local labour markets in which recently arrived migrants tend to cluster. If you're forced to compete against recently arrived migrants for low-paid and insecure jobs in the manual trades or the lower echelons of the service sector, it's difficult to set aside your personal troubles and cling on to the abstract calculations, often discussed in newspapers and on TV news broadcasts, that suggest immigrants make a significant overall contribution to the nation's economy.

So, we do not deny that racism among the white working class is growing. However, as social scientists, we began this project in the hope of uncovering the forces that appear to be driving this trend. For us it is not enough to simply repeat over and over again that we are against racism, and that people who express racist beliefs are bad and need to change. We are dedicated to the discovery of what's going on out there in the real world.

Why the left must change

The racism of today is a post-imperial racism rooted in global political economy and the absolute decline of traditional working-class work, security and status in the west. This is not simply the traditional racism that was primarily a product of imperialist colonial ideology. Where that was a racism of imaginary superiority, this is a racism of imagined inferiority that each day passes an affirming reality test. There are cultural issues at stake, but these develop in relation to this central economic issue. The sense of community dissolution and the gradual disappearance of the traditional culture are important, and they are experienced as such by millions of ordinary men and women across the country. It doesn't help at all when these processes are dismissed as irrelevant by academics and commentators who tell the working class to get over themselves, catch up with the rest of us, accept the cold and ahistorical world of western consumer culture, and eke out a new position of safety in the unforgiving global economy. More and more people today feel lost, rootless and set apart from the world. We know this. It's part of the way we live today. The solidity, security and continuity of traditional cultural life has disappeared. More and more people feel history leaving them behind. In the absence of a substantive political project capable of connecting these issues to their true cause – and amid the systematic silencing of any public talk about the possibility of such a project – these people look around for someone or something to blame.

There once existed a functional and committed left that sought to connect the economic and cultural frustrations of the multiethnic working class to their true cause. The mainstream political left today shows absolutely no desire to do this. It shows no desire to actually intervene in any effective way in the world in order to address the frustrations and pressures that blight so many working-class lives. The left today appears to believe that the very best it can hope for is to mitigate some of capitalism's worst effects by persuading government ministers to adopt new policy interventions geared towards removing blockages in the system as it presently exists. The virtual disappearance of a strident left willing to affect genuine change has altered the entire political spectrum. The anchor that held the entire system in place has been withdrawn, and as a result our political system has drifted gradually to the right. Liberalism has won. Socialism and one-nation conservatism are, at least for the moment, dead. The liberal left argues with the liberal right about the extent to which the government should tax individuals and corporations, but these arguments inevitably strike the precarious working class as sterile and forced because, ultimately, the liberal left agrees with the liberal right on everything bar the small details. Both groups speak with one voice on all issues related to global political economy, and it is only on the field of political economy that politicians can affect genuine structural change. Ultimately, our political system has been eroded, truncated and deprived of the substance it once had, and the workaday politics of Westminster appears stage-managed and bereft of the energy and innovation that might set us on a different course.

We have argued at some length that the exhaustion and decrepitude of the left today is the principal reason why so many of the white working class are moving to the right. The rise of the right is inextricably connected to the decline of the left. It is now time for the left to begin a thorough political and intellectual stock-check. The left must be honest enough to acknowledge the mistakes that have been made, and it must work tirelessly to reattach itself to its roots in the working class. If the left can't do this – if it remains lost in identity politics and dominated by right-on metropolitan liberals who appear totally unwilling to intervene in the economy to improve the fortunes of the working class – we will continue to drift gradually and inevitably into an era dominated by the political right.

References

Anderson, B. (1983) *Imagined communities*, London: Verso.

Barnosky, A. and Hardly, A. (2016) *Tipping point for Planet Earth*, London: Thomas Dunne Books.

Benjamin, W. (1996) *Selected writings, Vol 1 1, 1913-1926*, Cambridge, MA: Belknap Press.

Bollas, C. (1997) *Cracking up: The work of unconscious experience*, London: Routledge.

Busher, J. (2015) *The making of anti-Muslim protest*, London: Routledge.

Cohen, S. (2000) *States of denial*, Oxford: Polity.

Copsey, N. (2010) 'The English Defence League: Challenging our country and our values of social inclusion, fairness and equality', London: *Faith Matters*.

Cosslett, R.L. (2016a) 'If you're young and angry about the EU referendum, you're right to be', *The Guardian*, 24 June.

Cosslett, R.L (2016b) 'Family rifts over Brexit: "I can barely look at my parents"', *The Guardian*, 27 June.

Dave, P. (2006) *Visions of England*, Oxford: Berg.

Dorling, D. (2014) *Inequality and the 1%*, Bristol: Policy Press.

Dorling, D. (2015) *Injustice*, Bristol: Policy Press.

Elgot, J. (2016) 'Young Remain voters came out in force, but were outgunned', *The Guardian*, 4 June.

Ellis, A. (2015) *Men, masculinity and violence*, London: Routledge.

Fraser, I. (2016) 'Number of homes on the market at record low as Brexit uncertainty hits house prices', *The Telegraph*, 11 August.

Freud, S. (2001) *Complete psychological works of Sigmund Freud, Vol 14: On the history of the post psychoanalytic movement, Papers on metapsychology and other works*, London: Vintage.

Garland, J. and Treadwell, J. (2010) '"No Surrender to the Taliban!" Football hooliganism, Islamophobia and the rise of the English Defence League', *Papers from the British Criminology Conference 2010*, vol 10, pp 19-35.

Griffiths, S. (2014) *Engaging enemies: Hayek and the Left*, London: Rowman & Littlefield.

Hall, S. (2012) *Theorizing crime and deviance: A new perspective*, London: Sage.

Hall, S., Winlow, S. and Ancrum, C. (2008) *Criminal identities and consumer culture: Crime, exclusion and the new culture of narcissism*, Cullompton: Willan.

Harvey, D. (2011) *The enigma of capital*, London: Profile Books.

Hedges, C. (2011) *Death of the liberal class*, New York: Nation Books.

Heinberg, R. (2011) *The end of growth*, London: Clareview Books.

Hiscock, G. (2012) *Earth wars*, London: John Wiley & Sons.

Hoggart, R. (1969) *The uses of literacy*, London: Penguin.

Horsley, M. (2015) *The dark side of prosperity*, Farnham: Ashgate.

Jacoby, R. (2013) *Picture imperfect*, New York: Columbia University Press.

Jensen, T. and Tyler, I. (2015) '"Benefits broods": The cultural and political crafting of anti-welfare commonsense', *Critical Social Policy*, vol 35, no 4, pp 470-91.

Johnston, A. (2008) *Zizek's ontology: A transcendental materialist theory of subjectivity*, Boston, MA: Northwestern University Press.

Keen, S. (2011) *Debunking economics*, London: Zed Books.

Klare, M. (2001) *Resource wars*, New York: Metropolitan Books.

Klare, M. (2008) *Rising powers, shrinking planet*, London: Oneworld.

Krugman, P. (2013) *End this depression now!*, New York: Norton.

Lloyd, A. (2013) *Labour markets and identity on the post-industrial assembly line*, Farnham: Ashgate.

McKenzie, L. (2015) *Getting by*, Bristol: Policy Press.

McKenzie, L. (2016) 'Brexit is the only way the working class can change anything', *The Guardian*, 15 June.

Mendoza, K. (2015) *Austerity*, Oxford: New Internationalist.

Miles, S. (2015) *Retail and the artifice of social change*, London: Routledge.

O'Hara, M. (2015) *Austerity bites*, Bristol: Policy Press.

Owen, P. (2010) 'Ex-Treasury secretary Liam Byrne's note to his successor: there's no money left', *The Guardian*, 17 May.

Parenti, C. (2011) *Tropic of chaos*, London: Nation Books.

Perraudin, F. (2015) 'Labour risks turning into a sect, says Tristram Hunt', *The Guardian*, 2 November.

Piketty, T. (2014) *Capital in the twenty-first century*, Cambridge, MA: Harvard University Press.

Press Association (2015) 'Average UK household to be £10,000 in debt by end of 2016', *The Guardian*, 13 March.

Popper, K. (2011) *The open society and its enemies*, Abingdon: Routledge Classics.

Ranciere, J. (2010a) *Dissensus*, London: Continuum.

Ranciere, J. (2010b) *Chronicles of consensual times*, London: Continuum.

Raymen, T. (2015) 'Designing-in crime by designing-out the social? Situational crime prevention and the intensification of harmful subjectivities', *British Journal of Criminology*, doi: 10.1093/bjc/azv069.

Redhead, S. (2004) *Paul Virilio: Theorist for an accelerated culture*, Edinburgh: Edinburgh University Press.

Redhead, S. (2011) *We have never been postmodern*, Edinburgh: Edinburgh University Press.

Rifkin, J. (1995) *The end of work*, New York: Tarcher/Putnam.

Rodionova, Z. (2016) 'Brexit recession "could increase unemployment rate to equivalent of 500,000 lost jobs"', *The Independent*, 14 July.

Sassen, S. (1988) *The mobility of labour and capital*, Cambridge: Cambridge University Press.

Shaxson, N. (2012) *Treasure islands*, London: The Bodley Head.

Smith, O. (2014) *Contemporary adulthood and the night-time economy*, London: Palgrave Macmillan.

Smith, O. and Raymen, T. (2015) 'Shopping with violence: Black Friday sales in the British context', *Journal of Consumer Culture*, doi.1469540515611204.

Southwood, I. (2011) *Non-stop inertia*, London: Zero.

Stein, J. (2016) *The world of Marcus Garvey: Race and class in modern society*, Baton Rouge, LA: LSU Press.

Stewart, H. (2012) '£13tn hoard hidden from taxman by global elite', *The Guardian*, 21 July.

Stiglitz, J. (2010) *Freefall*, London: Penguin.

Therborn, G. (2014) *The killing fields of inequality*, Oxford: Polity Press.

Tilly, C. (2008) *Contentious performances*, Cambridge: Cambridge University Press.

Treadwell, J. and Garland, J. (2011) 'Masculinity, marginalization and violence: A case study of the English Defence League', *British Journal of Criminology*, vol 51, no 4, pp 621-34.

Treadwell, J., Briggs, D., Winlow, S. and Hall, S. (2013) 'Shopocalypse now: Consumer culture and the English riots of 2011', *British Journal of Criminology*, vol 53, no 1, pp 1-17.

Tyler, I. (2013) *Revolting subjects*, London: Zed Books.

UNHCR (UN Refugee Agency) (2015) 'Worldwide displacement hits all-time high as war and persecution increase', Geneva: UNHCR (www.unhcr.org/uk/news/latest/2015/6/558193896/worldwide-displacement-hits-all-time-high-war-persecution-increase.html).

Vale, P. (2016) 'Nicky Morgan to warn Brexit would create "lost generation" of young people', *Huffington Post*, 29 March.

Varoufakis, Y. (2013) *The global Minotaur*, London: Zed Books.

Wearden, G. and Fletcher, N. (2016) 'Brexit panic wipes $2 trillion off world markets', *The Guardian*, 24 June.

Whitehead, P. (2015) *Reconceptualising the moral economy of criminal justice*, London: Palgrave Macmillan.

Whitehead, P. and Crawshaw, P. (2013) 'Shaking the foundations: On the moral economy of criminal justice', *British Journal of Criminology*, vol 53, no 4, pp 588-604.

Wilford, H. (2003) *The CIA, the British Left and the Cold War: Calling the tune?*, London: Routledge.

Winlow, S. and Hall, S. (2006) *Violent night: Urban leisure and contemporary culture*, Oxford: Berg.

Winlow, S. and Hall, S. (2009) 'Living for the weekend: Youth identities in northeast England', *Ethnography*, vol 10, no 1, pp 91-113.

References

Winlow, S. and Hall, S. (2012) 'A predictably obedient riot: Post-politics, consumer culture, and the English riots of 2011', *Cultural Politics*, vol 8, no 3, pp 465–88.

Winlow, S. and Hall, S. (2013) *Rethinking social exclusion: The end of the social?*, London: Sage.

Winlow, S., Hall, S., Treadwell, J. and Briggs, D. (2015) *Riots and political protest: Notes from the post-political present*, London: Routledge.

Index